Table of Contents

Introduction to Volume 2

Welcome to Learn HTML 5, JavaScript and CSS (Launch Your Development Career) Volume 2.

If you are new to programming and you haven't read Volume 1, please check that book out first. You can see it at amazon (https://amzn.to/2M2HSYy).

Volume 1 will prepare you for what we are going to learn here. If you already understand the following concepts you will be fine to continue with this book:

LIST OF THINGS LEARNED IN VOLUME 1

- Basic history of HTML (how & why it was created)
- HTML Structure & Basics
- HTML Tags and Elements

- Using HTML W3C Validtor
- Basics of how web browsers work and how the JavaScript interpreter runs.
- CSS Selectors
- Selecting Elements using JavaScript and document.querySelector() and querySelectorAll.
- Create CSS Styles
- Link CSS into your HTML pages.
- Adding JavaScript to your pages.
- Basic JavaScript
- Creating and testing JavaScript using free resources at https://jsbin.com and https://codepen.io
- Creating and using Input controls in HTML (Select lists, textboxes, buttons, radio buttons, checkboxes, etc).

If you don't understand all of those things extremely well, then go ahead and work your way through Volume 1 of this book.   You can get it at amazon : https://amzn.to/2ZZipT4.

We start Volume 2 here on Day 37, because the first 36 days are covered in Volume 1.

Day 37

At this point (if you've followed through the previous 36 days of Volume 1) you know the basics about everything you need to know to begin writing a complete program.

I'm not saying that you know everything to go off and write every app you may imagine. I'm saying that you are now ready to put the things that you've learned together to make something larger.

That's what programming is all about: writing programs, automating tasks, creating solutions that people want or need. At times people get stuck on learning every detail of the programming language or technology they are learning before they ever begin building something. However, you'll find that many of those people get stuck dotting every i and crossing every t and forget to go out and build something.

There are some other things that programmer / technical people get stuck on too.

Technical Wars

You will find people in the tech industry are ready to go to war to defend :
1) Their language (JavaScript, C#, Python)
2) The frameworks they use (AngularJS, NodeJS, Svelte, React, etc)
3) Why one algorithm is so much better than another. Why you must do something a specific way.

Of course, there are good reasons to select one algorithm over another but just fighting about it all day doesn't get you any closer to your goal.

Best Tool To Solve the Problem

But we don't care about those things. We want to use the best tool to solve the problem. We want to use the tool that will help us get to the solution the easiest and create code that is the simplest to maintain and enhance.

Simplest Is Always Best

As the saying goes, "As simple as possible, but no simpler."
Imagine if we could build a complete website with only fifteen lines of code. That would be fantastic. That would make it so much easier to add features and fix bugs.

Think About Solutions At A High Level

Let's begin to think about what we want to create from a high level at first. Let's see if we can define 99% of all program functionality. Over all what does any program really do or provide to the user?

Every Software Solution

Here we are thinking about Application Software which means applications that are meant to be used by humans. There are other types of software (device drivers, services, etc) that automate other interactions which are oriented toward hardware and computer systems interaction instead of a human user.

The types of applications we are talking about provide the following:

- Some type of User Interface (UI)
  - The UI (User Interface) may be complex visual elements like we've seen with buttons and text boxes etc. but it could also just be the command-line (aka console or terminal) which allows a user to enter text commands.
  - The Interface provides a way for the user to interact with the program. With a static (unchanging) web page, this could just be allowing the user to read the text of the web site.
- A way for user to interact with data
  - Users often want to create, read, update, or delete (CRUD) data within the app. For example if you create a daily journal app the user will want to create entries. Later she may need to update an entry to add something to it. At some point in the future she may need to go back and read the entry again. Finally, she may decide to delete the entry if she no longer has use for it.
  - Where is the data stored? This is a big decision we have to make when we are creating our programs. Data may be stored in a file on the user's computer or in a database on the server. Deciding where data will be stored is a big part of designing our apps. There are also security challenges related to storing data because a regular HTML app will not have access to the user's file system.

The App We Are Going to Develop

We are going to build an app that will allow the user to use (copy/paste) and manage emojis.

Windows has an emoji pad type of thing that allows you to copy an emoji. You can get to it by holding your WindowsKey and pressing the comma. It looks like the following:

The bottom toolbar menu allows you to see different types of emojis. The clock is the recent items. The face is the list of face expressions, etc.

We'll definitely steal from this idea. That's right, just like Steve Jobs said, "Good artists copy, great artists steal."

With Added Features

However, we will add a feature which allows the user to add new emojis for later use. The set of emojis in the Windows 10 emoji app are baked in. You can't add new ones and Microsoft controls when new ones are added.

Pre-made CSS

We are going to use some pre-made CSS via a CSS library named Bootstrap. It's really named Twitter Bootstrap, because I guess these styles were originally used to design Twitter.

Our final app will look something like the following:

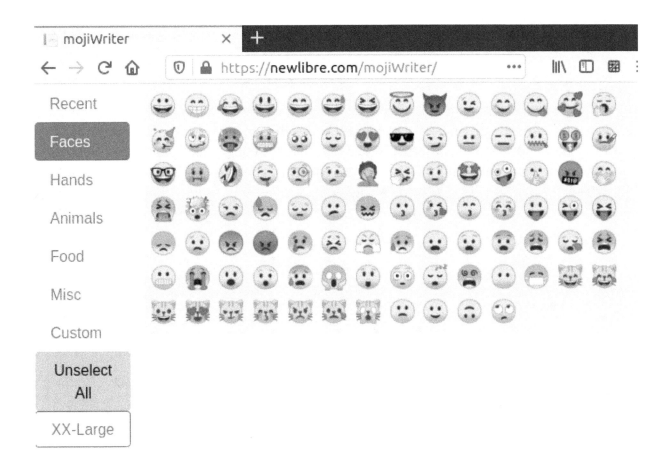

You can even try it out at my web site right now if you like: https://newlibre.com/mojiWriter

We're going to do all of this. However, before we get started, we need to take a little detour into Source Control.

What Is Source Control?

Source Control is an application that helps us keep track of the changes we make in our code. The code we write is called the Source or Source Code. It is the source of what the application can do. Source control will track every change you make to your code. This allows us to try more things without losing work that we've already done. This type of software is also called a Version Control System because you can control the versions of your code that you are using.

Why Do We Need To Use Source Control?

You will see that there are times when you want to try changing something in your code, but you're not sure if the changes are going to work or if you really want to go in a certain direction with your design. With source control you can commit (or check in) your code. The commit takes a snapshot of exactly what the code looks like. Then you can work on your changes and try them out. If they don't work out, you simply revert back to your original commit code and you've lost nothing but some time.

Git Version Control

We will go into the details of how to get started using Git tomorrow. Some of it will be annoying and feel like overhead that isn't going to pay you back. But, keep in mind, real software devs use Version Control Software. This is one of the milestones that you need to pass in order to be a real software dev. I will do my best to convince you (and someday you will see for yourself) that version control software is a dev's best friend.

Day 38

Installing Git

The most direct way to install Git on your Windows computer is to go to the official Git site:
https://git-scm.com/download/win

When you get there you'll see something like the following:

Downloading Git

Your download is starting...

You are downloading the latest (**2.30.0**) **64-bit** version of **Git for Windows**. This is the most recent maintained build. It was released **13 days ago**, on 2021-01-14.

Click here to download manually, **if your download hasn't started.**

Other Git for Windows downloads

Git for Windows Setup
32-bit Git for Windows Setup.

64-bit Git for Windows Setup.

Git for Windows Portable ("thumbdrive edition")
32-bit Git for Windows Portable.

64-bit Git for Windows Portable.

The current source code release is version 2.30.0. If you want the newer version, you can build it from the source code.

Most likely you are running a 64-bit Win10 OS so that is probably the one you want.

Once you download it you need to run the program and walk through the wizard to install Git on your machine.

Once you get it all installed, you'll see a new icon when you click your Windows Start button. It'll look something like the following (Git Bash).

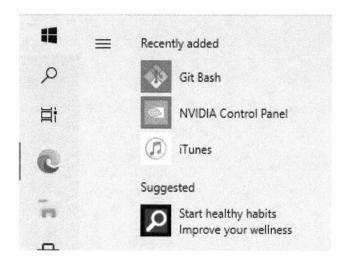

Git Bash is a Linux bash (Bourne Again Shell) terminal. That means when you run it you will see a console and that console will support Linux Bash commands.

Yes, this means that you can run shell commands as if you are running a Linux terminal.

Here's what it is going to look like when you run the program.

So basically when you run this new git thing, you are going to be looking at a terminal window. Notice that the title bar says, "MINGW64" and provides a path.

That stands for Minimalist Gnu for Windows (64-bit). Gnu is a set of open source tools that were created for Unix/Linux environments. You can learn more about it at :
https://en.wikipedia.org/wiki/MinGW

Not Just Git

The point here is that running this on your Windows box is basically like running a Linux terminal. This means that not just Git was installed, but an environment for running Git as a Linux program.

Why Is This Important?

The reason this is important to know is that you are going to need to know some basics of Linux to get around in bash (shell). What is a shell? It is an interface to the underlying Operating System. One of the interfaces allows you to interact with the file system.

Ubuntu / Linux

If you are running Ubuntu (as I am) then Git is most likely already installed.
Just open a terminal and type : $ git --version

You should see something like the following if you already have it:

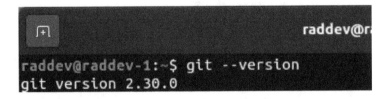

Git Bash: Quick YouTube Video

You can watch a quick video I created and uploaded to YouTube which shows Git Bash in action and creating a directory in your user home directory at: https://youtu.be/EajeSy3g8Rw
I also explain how to properly pin Git Bash to your task bar. Win10 messes up your path if you don't do it the correct way.

Determine Which Directory You Are In

Print Working Directory (pwd)

Try the following command. The $ is your prompt so don't type that.
Just type everything that follows the $ and then press <ENTER>
$ pwd

```
1rade@DESKTOP-B1PSFKN MINGW64 ~
$ pwd
/c/Users/1rade

1rade@DESKTOP-B1PSFKN MINGW64 ~
$ |
```

You can see I'm in my user directory.
If you haven't done anything else you probably see your user directory listed.

Notice the Use of Slashes

Notice that Linux lists directories a bit differently than Windows does.
If you run the pwd command from a Windows prompt you would see:
c:\Users\1rade

Directory Terminators Are Different

Windows uses backslashes \ as the directory terminator.
Linux uses slashes / as the directory terminator.

Also, windows refers to drives as [DriveLetter]: c: or d:
However, Linux refers to drives as /c or /d etc.

List Directories and Files

The main way to list the directories and files is using the ls command.
Try the following:
$ ls -al

That command means list -a (all) files and directories in the current directory and -l means use long listing format.

```
ta/Roaming/Microsoft/Windows/Network Shortcuts'/
drwxr-xr-x 1 1rade 197609       0 Jan 28 15:06  OneDrive/
drwxr-xr-x 1 1rade 197609       0 Oct 10 12:12  Pictures/
lrwxrwxrwx 1 1rade 197609      66 Oct 10 12:07  PrintHood -> '/c/Users/1rade/App
Data/Roaming/Microsoft/Windows/Printer Shortcuts'/
lrwxrwxrwx 1 1rade 197609      55 Oct 10 12:07  Recent -> /c/Users/1rade/AppData
/Roaming/Microsoft/Windows/Recent/
drwxr-xr-x 1 1rade 197609       0 Oct 10 12:10  'Saved Games'/
drwxr-xr-x 1 1rade 197609       0 Oct 10 12:12  Searches/
lrwxrwxrwx 1 1rade 197609      55 Oct 10 12:07  SendTo -> /c/Users/1rade/AppData
/Roaming/Microsoft/Windows/SendTo/
lrwxrwxrwx 1 1rade 197609      59 Oct 10 12:07  'Start Menu' -> '/c/Users/1rade/A
ppData/Roaming/Microsoft/Windows/Start Menu'/
lrwxrwxrwx 1 1rade 197609      58 Oct 10 12:07  Templates -> /c/Users/1rade/AppD
ata/Roaming/Microsoft/Windows/Templates/
drwxr-xr-x 1 1rade 197609       0 Oct 28 15:30  Videos/
drwxr-xr-x 1 1rade 197609       0 Oct 10 17:12  dev/
-rw-r--r-- 1 1rade 197609  393216 Oct 10 12:07  ntuser.dat.LOG1
-rw-r--r-- 1 1rade 197609  434176 Oct 10 12:07  ntuser.dat.LOG2
-rw-r--r-- 1 1rade 197609      20 Oct 10 12:07  ntuser.ini
drwxr-xr-x 1 1rade 197609       0 Jan 27 15:09  utils/

1rade@DESKTOP-B1PSFKN MINGW64 ~
$ |
```

The first letter you see in white text is the type of item that is found.
Ones that have a d are directories.
Ones that have a l are links (not important right now).
Ones that have a - are files.
You can see that OneDrive/ is a directory.
You can see that there is a file named ntuser.dat.LOG1
The last directory listed is named utils/

Make Directory

A directory is simply a folder that can hold one or more files. A directory can contain other directories too. Creating a directory allows us to organize our files into projects.

Let's make a couple of new directories so we can use the same directory names as we go through the following work.

Project Directory

Since you are in your user directory, let's create a new project directory that we will simply name dev. Use the mkdir command to create a new directory.

$ mkdir dev

Now we want to change directory into that directory.

Change Directory
Let's try a change directory. This will be different on your system, because you won't have the same directory names.
$ cd dev

Once you run those two commands (mkdir dev and cd dev) your prompt will look something like the following:

```
1rade@DESKTOP-B1PSFKN MINGW64 ~
$ mkdir dev

1rade@DESKTOP-B1PSFKN MINGW64 ~
$ cd dev

1rade@DESKTOP-B1PSFKN MINGW64 ~/dev
$
```

Notice at the end you see that ~/dev   That is indicating the current directory you are in. The ~ means user home which is your user directory. So in my case ~ or /c/Users/1rade are the same thing.

~/dev is the same thing on my machine as /c/Users/1rade/dev

You could do all of this in File Explorer. The directory would look like the following:

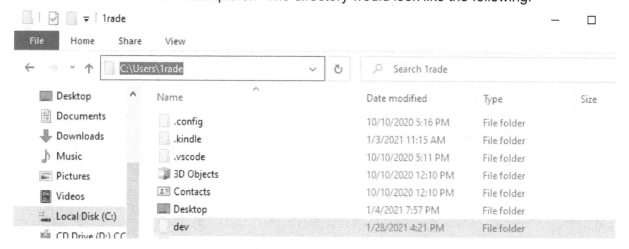

See the C: drive on the left. And under that we have Users\1rade and finally the dev directory.

Here's another view if you expand the directories on the left under the c: drive.

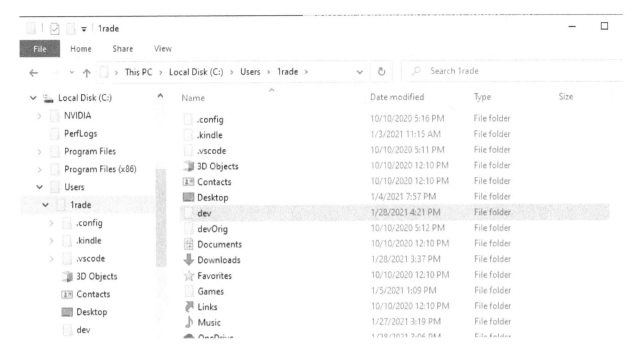

The point here is that it is all the same thing and you are just seeing a more limited view at the terminal (in git bash).

Make A Directory For Our Project

Switch back to your git bash terminal again and we are going to add a directory for our new project. We are going to name it /moji. I just place the slash there to indicate it is a folder.

In the git bash terminal you should still be in your dev directory.
Run the following commands:
$ mkdir moji
$ cd moji

This will create the new directory and then it will put you inside the directory.

```
1rade@DESKTOP-B1PSFKN MINGW64 ~/dev
$ mkdir moji

1rade@DESKTOP-B1PSFKN MINGW64 ~/dev
$ cd moji

1rade@DESKTOP-B1PSFKN MINGW64 ~/dev/moji
$
```

Again, you can see you are now in the moji directory because it is listed in yellow.

This has been a lot of learning and work today, but you are progressing through the tools that will make you a professional developer.

Let's take a break until tomorrow, but go back and try to create another new directory in your dev directory.

How Would You Change Back To Dev Directory?

There are three ways you can do this:
1. $ cd ~/dev
2. $ cd ..
3. $ cd /c/Users/1rade/dev

The first one is the shortcut method of typing the user home directory (~) instead of longer path. The second one moves you up (or back) one directory. That .. (two dots) means go to parent directory from the directory you are currently in. Since you are in ~/dev/moji moving up one directory will move you into the ~/dev directory.

The third one uses the long absolute path to the user home directory.

Hint: If You Get Really Confused About Where You Are

If you get really confused about where you are, then simply close the Git Bash window (application) and then go back and start the application again.

When the app starts you will be back in your user home directory.

The other guaranteed way to get back to your user home directory is to use the following command:

$ cd ~

Note: There is a space between the cd command and the tilde ~.

Homework: Create New Directory Under Dev

Once you get into your ~/dev directory, try creating a new directory named test.

Day 39

You're ready for this chapter, once you've successfully:
1. installed Git
2. created your new dev directory under your user home (~)

Now we want to create a new directory named moji
This will be the directory which holds our project.
Later on, we will be creating additional directories under this main moji directory so that we can organize the files in our project.

As you gain more experience you'll find your own way of organizing your projects. Organization using folders (directories) is just a convention* that we use to make our lives easier.

*convention -- Merriam-Webster.com defines it this way: a general agreement about basic principles or procedures.

For now I'll show you specific folders (directories) to create so we can match up what we're doing as we develop our moji manager application.

After you open Git Bash and cd (change directory) into your dev directory, we want to create a directory named moji which will hold all the files and directories for our main project.

```
 MINGW64:/c/Users/1rade/dev/moji

1rade@mobidev MINGW64 ~/dev
$ mkdir moji

1rade@mobidev MINGW64 ~/dev
$ cd moji

1rade@mobidev MINGW64 ~/dev/moji
$ ls -al
total 0
drwxr-xr-x 1 1rade 197609 0 Feb 14 10:21 ./
drwxr-xr-x 1 1rade 197609 0 Feb 14 10:21 ../

1rade@mobidev MINGW64 ~/dev/moji
$
```

First we use mkdir to create the moji directory.
Next, we cd into that directory so we can create two more directories inside it.

You can see I also did a listing (ls -al) from inside the moji directory but there is nothing in it at this point except the two directories named dot and dotdot (. and ..).

Those oddly named directories represent the parent (of moji) named dotdot (..) and the the current directory named dot (.).

Parent Directory (.)

If you wanted to move up one directory from any other directory it would not be possible without the .. directory. There wouldn't be an easy way to reference it if it didn't exist. We'll learn more about the current directory later (.).

For now let's continue creating the other directories we'll use for our moji project.

```
1rade@mobidev MINGW64 ~/dev/moji
$ mkdir css

1rade@mobidev MINGW64 ~/dev/moji
$ ls -al
total 0
drwxr-xr-x 1 1rade 197609 0 Feb 14 10:30 ./
drwxr-xr-x 1 1rade 197609 0 Feb 14 10:21 ../
drwxr-xr-x 1 1rade 197609 0 Feb 14 10:30 css/
drwxr-xr-x 1 1rade 197609 0 Feb 14 10:30 js/
```

You can see that I created two new directories:
1. js - to hold our JavaScript files
2. css -- to hold our Cascading StyleSheet files

Visual Studio Code (VSC)

Now that we've created all of those folders and become a bit more familiar with the git bash terminal (console or command line) let's open up Visual Studio Code (or your favorite editor) and open this folder so we can easily create our project files.

Over in VSC we want to open up the project folder because VSC helps us to view all of the files in our project. You'll need to go to File...Open Folder...

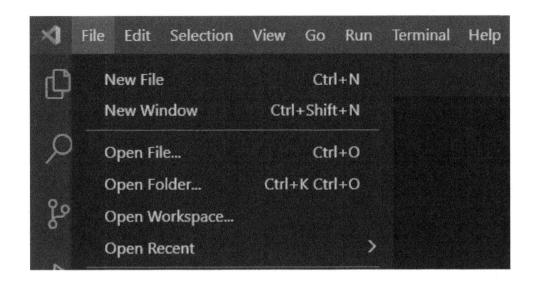

After the Windows File/Folder Open dialog starts up you'll want to navigate to your c:\users\<username>\dev\moji\ directory and click the [Select Folder] button.

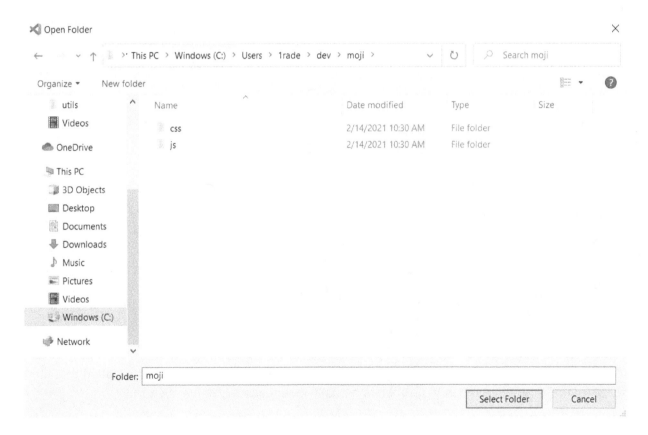

When you do that Visual Studio Code will now show you the project folder and subfolders but there isn't anything else listed (since we haven't added any files) and it looks a bit odd.

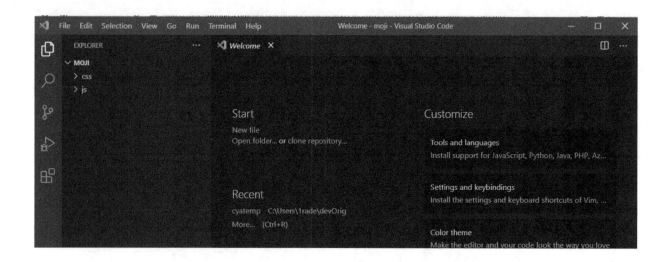

Add First File To Project and Git

Now, we're ready to create our first file to the project and Git.

Make sure you have selected the MOJI folder on the left side of VSC.
It will get a blue highlight box around it when you've selected it properly (see next image).

Next, you'll want to click the [New File] icon (shown highlighted in red in next image).

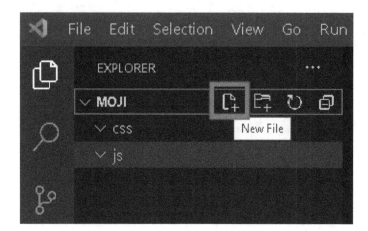

When you click that button a new file will be created in the MOJI folder. It is interesting that the folder name is uppercased in VSC but it is actually lowercase in the file system.

Bug In Visual Studio Code

I discovered (as I followed these steps myself) that there is basically a bug in VSC that causes the new file to be added to one of the subfolders (\css or \js) every time you create it.

Since this is true. I'm going to make the project directory available for download from the GitHub source for this book.

GitHub Clone

Because of this bug, I'm now going to show you how to clone the GitHub repository for this book so you will have all of the code on your local drive so you can use any of the files any time you need to. This make using this book a lot easier.

The clone command simply means to create a local copy of the remote GitHub repository. Repository is just a big word which means storage location.

Let's switch back to Git Bash so we can clone this repository to your ~/dev directory. It's very easy and it will pull all of the code into a local folder named \LaunchYDC (Launch Your Dev Career).

Clone LaunchYDC

Make sure you cd (change directory) back to your home\dev directory. You can use the following command to get there:
$ cd ~\dev

Once you're in that directory go ahead and run the git command that will copy the entire repository to a local directory:
$ git clone https://github.com/raddevus/LaunchYDC

MINGW64:/c/Users/1rade/dev

```
1rade@mobidev MINGW64 ~/dev
$ git clone https://github.com/raddevus/LaunchYDC
```

Notice that the link to the GitHub repo is clickable. If you click it, your browser will take you to the actual repository on GitHub. GitHub is not the same thing as Git. Git is the VCS (Version Control Software). GitHub is a web storage area (owned by Microsoft) which allows us to store our Git repositories to make them public (so others can get to them).

Once you hit <ENTER> and the clone begins and completes you'll see something like the following:

```
1rade@mobidev MINGW64 ~/dev
$ git clone https://github.com/raddevus/LaunchYDC
Cloning into 'LaunchYDC'...
remote: Enumerating objects: 57, done.
remote: Counting objects: 100% (57/57), done.
remote: Compressing objects: 100% (35/35), done.
remote: Total 57 (delta 20), reused 51 (delta 17), pack-reused 0
Receiving objects: 100% (57/57), 14.68 KiB | 69.00 KiB/s, done.
Resolving deltas: 100% (20/20), done.

1rade@mobidev MINGW64 ~/dev
$
```

List everything in your ~/dev directory and you'll see you have a new folder named /LaunchYDC
$ ls -al

```
1rade@mobidev MINGW64 ~/dev
$ ls -al
total 12
drwxr-xr-x 1 1rade 197609 0 Feb 14 11:45 ./
drwxr-xr-x 1 1rade 197609 0 Feb 14 11:31 ../
drwxr-xr-x 1 1rade 197609 0 Feb 14 11:45 LaunchYDC/
drwxr-xr-x 1 1rade 197609 0 Feb 14 11:18 moji/

1rade@mobidev MINGW64 ~/dev
$ |
```

To get the beginning files we need for this project you can open file explorer and navigate to
c:\users\<username>\dev\LaunchYDC\volume2\moji-1

SpecialFolders In Windows 10

If you're running Windows 10 you can get to the folder in File Explorer by using the following special folder. Just copy it and paste it into the top of File Explorer and press <ENTER>
%userprofile%\dev\LaunchYDC\volume2\moji-1

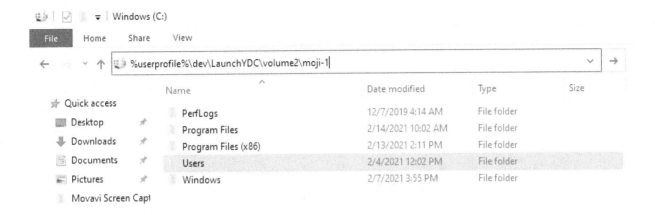

No matter where you are in the folder system, this will take you to the moj-1 folder (as long as you've cloned it properly onto your computer).

%userprofile% is a special environment variable that windows can access, which points to your specific users directory.

Why All This Extra? This is IT

It may seem as if I take you down some extra side streets on our way to your Development Career. However, these extras are the things that will take you years to learn on your own. If you learn them now, along the way, you will be far stronger in your IT (Information Technology) career.

These things are a part of IT and computers that get ignored a lot but they are what provides you with the ability to really do your work. The file system has been a part of computers since the beginning and understanding it from many angles (terminal, windows explorer, etc) makes you stronger and helps you understand concepts that will make you speak about the work you do much more fluidly. When you get into an interview you may be ask to show how to do certain things. If you're stuck on figuring out how to even open a file the interview is not going to go well.

Everything you learn here is making you a stronger candidate for every position you will hold in IT.

Copy All Files From moji-1

Once you've followed all of the previous steps all you have to do is copy all of the files (and folders) in the moji-1 directory and paste them into our main ~/dev/moji directory.

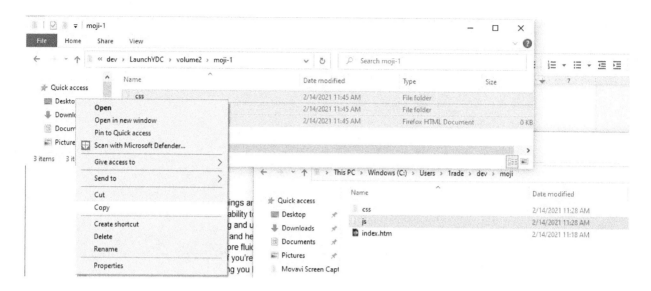

Copy the files in the moji-1 folder and past them into our moji folder.
If you had already created some of the folders or files, no worries, just tell the system to [Replace the files in the destination] and you'll have everything we need to get started.

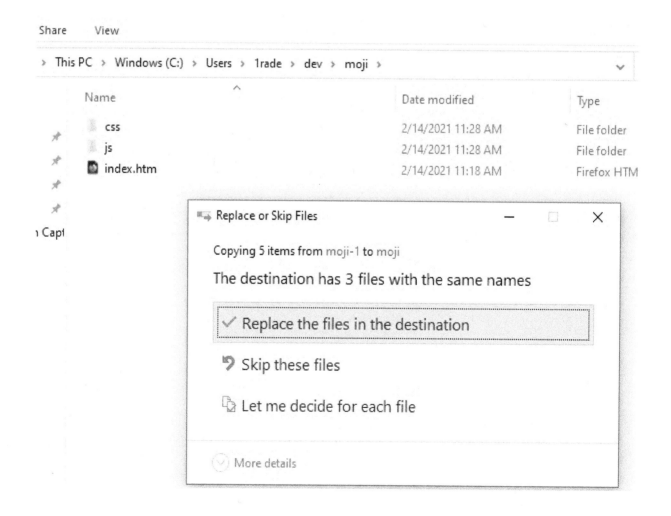

Finally, Create Our Git Repository

We are finally ready to create our Git Repository. It's very easy, but first we need to move back to Git bash since that is where we run our git commands.

The first thing we want to do is make sure we are in our ~/dev/moji project directory in git bash. Use the following command to make sure you are there.
$ cd ~/dev/moji

Confirm You Have Everything

Let's use a new option on the ls command to display all the folders and files under the ~/dev/moji (current) directory.
We are adding a new letter to the end of our familiar ls -al command. In this case we want to use a capital R which tells the ls command to Recurse through all subdirectories. Recursion means to do a thing repeatedly. So in this case the ls command will repeatedly list each subdirectory it finds.
Run the following command
$ ls -alR

```
 MINGW64:/c/Users/1rade/dev/moji

1rade@mobidev MINGW64 ~/dev/moji
$ ls -alR
.:
total 0
drwxr-xr-x 1 1rade 197609 0 Feb 14 11:18 ./
drwxr-xr-x 1 1rade 197609 0 Feb 14 11:45 ../
drwxr-xr-x 1 1rade 197609 0 Feb 14 11:28 css/
-rw-r--r-- 1 1rade 197609 0 Feb 14 11:45 index.htm
drwxr-xr-x 1 1rade 197609 0 Feb 14 11:28 js/

./css:
total 0
drwxr-xr-x 1 1rade 197609 0 Feb 14 11:28 ./
drwxr-xr-x 1 1rade 197609 0 Feb 14 11:18 ../
-rw-r--r-- 1 1rade 197609 0 Feb 14 11:45 main.css

./js:
total 0
drwxr-xr-x 1 1rade 197609 0 Feb 14 11:28 ./
drwxr-xr-x 1 1rade 197609 0 Feb 14 11:18 ../
-rw-r--r-- 1 1rade 197609 0 Feb 14 11:45 main.js

1rade@mobidev MINGW64 ~/dev/moji
$
```

Notice that it lists each directory name and then the files and folders in that directory.
The first directory it checks is the current (.) directory.
Next you can see it checks the ./css (css under the current directory).
Finally, it lists the ./js directory and you can see that we have three files in the three different directories.

1. ./index.htm
2. ./css/main.css
3. ./js/main.js

If yours looks similar then you are ready to create the git repository.

Since this has been a lot to work through today, we will continue that work tomorrow.

Day 40

Creating a Git repository is very easy.
All we need to do is use git to initialize the project directory.

From the ~/dev/moji directory run the following command.

$ git init

```
1rade@mobidev MINGW64 ~/dev/moji
$ git init
Initialized empty Git repository in C:/Users/1rade/dev/moji/.git/

1rade@mobidev MINGW64 ~/dev/moji (main)
$
```

After the command runs successfully it will tell you "Initialized empty Git repository in ~/dev/moji/.git/

That last directory is named .git and this is where git stores information about the repository.

The existence of that directory can also be an indication that the folder contains a git repository.

.git Is A Hidden Directory

However, if you attempt to view the directory in Windows File Explorer, most likely you will ont be able to see it. That's because the directory is marked as hidden, since it is not a directory that you should alter manually.

If you really wanted to see the directory in File Explorer you could change the View option so that it will show up. Just select the option in File Explorer shown in the next image.

So far we have only created an empty repository though so nothing is being tracked by Git yet.

To begin using Git we will need to add files to the repository first.

But, before we do that, let's see what Git thinks about the current state.
To do that we run the git status command.

$ git status

```
1rade@mobidev MINGW64 ~/dev/moji (main)
$ git status
On branch main

No commits yet

Untracked files:
  (use "git add <file>..." to include in what will be committed)
        css/
        index.htm
        js/

nothing added to commit but untracked files present (use "git add" to track)

1rade@mobidev MINGW64 ~/dev/moji (main)
$
```

You can see the following:
1. we are on a branch named main
2. We have not committed anything yet (we commit to "save" our changes into the git repository which tracks every change we make)
3. Git recognizes untracked files that are in the current directory and all subdirs
4. Git gives us an idea of how to start tracking files --- add them with git add

Add Files to Git

To add all of the files in the current directory (.) and files in all subdirectories to our git repo we we want to run the following command:

$ git add .

Notice that after the add command there is a space and a dot (.).

Run that command.

After you run that command git doesn't tell anything if it succeeded so go ahead and run the git status command again.

$ git status

```
1rade@mobidev MINGW64 ~/dev/moji (main)
$ git add .

1rade@mobidev MINGW64 ~/dev/moji (main)
$ git status
On branch main

No commits yet

Changes to be committed:
  (use "git rm --cached <file>..." to unstage)
        new file:   css/main.css
        new file:   index.htm
        new file:   js/main.js


1rade@mobidev MINGW64 ~/dev/moji (main)
$ |
```

We still see that there are no commits yet. We have only added the files to the repo in a staging area. The files are not added to the repo until we commit them.

Let's go and ahead and commit the files with the following command.

$ git commit -a -m "Adding initial files after repo creation."

That command takes two required parameters.
1. -a (all files -- commit all files that are staged)
2. -m (message (begin and end marked by double-quotes) which is used as a comment for work that was completed)

```
1rade@mobidev MINGW64 ~/dev/moji (main)
$ git commit -a -m "Adding initial files after repo creation."
[main (root-commit) 6465f0c] Adding initial files after repo creation.
 3 files changed, 0 insertions(+), 0 deletions(-)
 create mode 100644 css/main.css
 create mode 100644 index.htm
 create mode 100644 js/main.js

1rade@mobidev MINGW64 ~/dev/moji (main)
$ |
```

You can see that the three files were added to the repo.

What Does Adding Files To Repo Do?

Now those files will be watched by git so that any changes will be tracked and you will be able to ask git what the changes were. I'll explain this better in just a moment. But, first, let's go run a status on the repo again.

$ git status

```
1rade@mobidev MINGW64 ~/dev/moji (main)
$ git status
On branch main
nothing to commit, working tree clean

1rade@mobidev MINGW64 ~/dev/moji (main)
$
```

Git tells you that there are no changes and there is nothing to commit (since we last committed these files).

If Anything Changes, Git Status Will Tell Us

If we had added a file to any of the existing (or newly created) directories or if we had changed any of the three existing files (index.htm, css/main.css, js/main.js) then git would've told us about the changes.

You will see that this is a very valuable thing in software development because then you don't have to wonder why something suddenly stopped working. If something stops working you can look at what changed before and after and then work your way through what the problem is. Without git, it becomes incumbent upon you and your memory to remember what changed. If a project is very large at all that can be entirely impossible.

The Understand the Benefit You Have To Try It

To really understand the benefits you really have to try it. So let's finally make some changes to our project files and examine what git knows.

Add the following code (HTML) to the index.htm file in your moji project.

```
<!DOCTYPE html>
<html lang="en">
  <head>
      <title>moji: manage your emojis</title>
      <meta charset="utf-8">
  </head>
  <body>
      <h1>Moji</h1>
      <p>Manage your emojis!</p>
  </body>
</html>
```

It will look something like the following in VSC:

Make sure you save the file and then go back to git bash and check the status.

$ git status

It now tells you that index.htm has been modified.

Viewing a Diff On the File

Git also helps us see what actually changed in the file. This will be a bit odd because the file was empty and now has the HTML we added, but let's run the diff command.

$ git diff

```
1rade@mobidev MINGW64 ~/dev/moji (main)
$ git diff
diff --git a/index.htm b/index.htm
index e69de29..598c57e 100644
--- a/index.htm
+++ b/index.htm
@@ -0,0 +1,11 @@
+<!DOCTYPE html>
+<html lang="en">
+        <head>
+                <title>moji: manage your emojis</title>
+                <meta charset="utf-8">
+        </head>
+        <body>
+         <h1>Moji</h1>
+                <p>Manage your emojis!</p>
+        </body>
+</html>
\ No newline at end of file

1rade@mobidev MINGW64 ~/dev/moji (main)
$
```

Viewing the diff information can take a bit of getting used to so don't feel overwhelmed by all of that. Basically the lines that are green and have a + symbol are lines that are now in the file.

Let's commit this and then we'll go back and change something small so you can really see a good example of a diff.

Commit the changes now. Remember you can add any comment you want to add.

$ git commit -a -m "added initial html."

```
1rade@mobidev MINGW64 ~/dev/moji (main)
$ git commit -a -m "added initial html."
[main 2bd7b85] added initial html.
 1 file changed, 11 insertions(+)

1rade@mobidev MINGW64 ~/dev/moji (main)
$ |
```

Get An Idea Of What Has Changed: Examine Log

Let's take a look at the Git log now and you will see that it will list the commits and the commit messages that we've added so far. These can be really helpful if you use good commit messages so you can track what you've done in your project.

Run the following command and take a close look at the output.

$ git log

```
1rade@mobidev MINGW64 ~/dev/moji (main)
$ git log
commit 2bd7b854c4b6e482c4a70a327941bf0d78260512 (HEAD -> main)
Author: raddevus <1radeutsch1@gmailc.om>
Date:   Sun Feb 14 15:16:01 2021 -0500

    added initial html.

commit 6465f0c06237b85ce392f203d662fe991ea42129
Author: raddevus <1radeutsch1@gmailc.om>
Date:   Sun Feb 14 14:45:52 2021 -0500

    Adding initial files after repo creation.

1rade@mobidev MINGW64 ~/dev/moji (main)
$
```

The commits are listed in reverse chronological order so that the newest will be the one showing at the top.

The first thing you see in the yellow text is the commit revision value which allows you to refer to this exact commit if needed. You also see the HEAD -> main which means we are currently on the main branch of the code. Branching is a bit more of an advanced topic that we will cover later.

Notice also that you see the user who did the commit (raddevus) and the date and time that the commit was made. Finally you see your original commit message that was originally added when the commit was made. All of this info can really help us in the future when we are attempting to fix a bug or find out why something went wrong.

Make A Small Change, Examine Diff

Let's go make a small change to our index.htm and see how helpful git diff can be.

Here's our new HTML for the index.htm.

```
<!DOCTYPE html>
<html lang="en">
    <head>
        <title>moji: manage your emojis</title>
        <meta charset="utf-8">
    </head>
    <body>
```

```
        <h1>Moji</h1>
         <p>Manage all emojis!</p>
         <p>This is a new paragraph</p>
      </body>
</html>
```

I've altered the word "your" so that it is now "all"
I've also added the new <p> paragraph.

Save the changes and let's switch back to git bash and run git diff.

$git diff

Now git diff gives us something a bit more meaningful than the previous comparison to an empty file.

In this case, we can see that the first line (red with the leading - symbol) was removed. It was replaced with the line that follows (green with leading + symbol).

Finally, the other green line with leading + symbol was also added. That gives us a much better idea of what happened with the file and now we can decide if we want to commit the changes or not. If they are good changes then we are ready to commit. If not we can go make necessary changes and come back again.

Let's throw these changes away! This will be a bit like magic, because you will see that git can simply get rid of these changes and replace them with what you previously checked in.

Git Checkout: You Can Throw Changes Away

Since I don't really care about these changes let's go ahead and get rid of them. This can be very helpful if your file gets changed and you don't want the changes.

If Your Cat Runs Across Your Keyboard

Suppose your cat runs across your keyboard while you're away.

Normally you might not know what the code originally looked like. But with Git you do.

You'd just go out and do a $ git diff and you'd examine the changes. Then, since you don't want to keep the changes the Fluffy made to your file, go ahead and check out the original from the repo.
Just keep in mind that since the changes Fluffy made were not saved anywhere they will be gone forever. Git will overwrite them with the original file when you run the following command.

Go ahead and do it now.

$ git checkout index.htm

```
1rade@mobidev MINGW64 ~/dev/moji (main)
$ git checkout index.htm
Updated 1 path from the index

1rade@mobidev MINGW64 ~/dev/moji (main)
$ git status
On branch main
nothing to commit, working tree clean

1rade@mobidev MINGW64 ~/dev/moji (main)
$ |
```

You can see that git tells you: "Updated 1 path from the index" which is git's way of telling you that it updated the file from the original code.

Now when you do run $ git status git tells you you are one branch main and there is nothing to commit.
That's because your index.htm is now reverted to the one that was previously checked int.

Let's prove that by switching back to VSC and taking a look.

It's back to the original.

Git Is A Powerful Tool

Git is actually quite easy to use and you'll get better at it as you go. However, it is a really powerful tool because now you can worry a lot less about losing changes that you have made or about making changes that won't quite work. Since git is sitting there tracking the changes you make you won't ever lose anything and you'll be able to examine the changes you make very closely.

Git Philosophy: Commit Early, Commit Often

However, if you don't commit your changes then git cannot track them.
This is why it is so important to follow the Git Philosophy:

Commit early, commit often

Git can only track what you commit so make sure you commit a lot. Commits don't cost you anything, so make sure you commit as often as possible. Commits can be reverted by checking out earlier revisions (using revision numbers).

Git : Creates A Journal of What You Did

Remember to commit your code as much as possible and you'll find that you have a journal of what you did to create your code.

Git : It's A Professional's Tool

Git is a tool that makes you stand out as a professional. You don't have to know everything about Git, but you do need to know the things that you've learned in these short chapters and a little bit more that you'll learn in the future. Learning Git is one of the steps to turning into a professional developer. Not all developer's use VCS (Version Control Systems) but those who do not are not professionals (even if they are working in the industry). Using Git is like the carpenter who uses a hammer or a nail gun. You would never meet a carpenter who says, "well, I don't like to use hammers or nail guns."

Now that you know the basics of Git you are moving ahead of the crowd of wannabe devs who don't use it. We will continue to use it throughout this book (and all Volumes of Launch Your Dev Career).

Now, we need to determine what we are actually building. We have to have some idea of what we want the final product to be. Tomorrow we'll take a look at the process that has been used in the past to create software and we'll examine the newer alternative.

Day 41

Knowing what you're supposed to be building is a big part of developing software. If you waste your time adding features that no one wants it doesn't help your software at all.

Software Requirements

Gathering software requirements is one of the most boring things in the entire world. In the past, it was always difficult to find people who :
1. Wanted to gather requirements for their main job
2. Were good at gathering requirements
3. Had a process for gathering requirements

Other problems occurred too. Often the project wouldn't begin until the Requirements Gathering Phase was completely over. A lot of time (and money via worker's salaries) got invested into gathering requirements so later on no one wanted to go back and rework the requirements.

This became a part of the Software Development Methodology (working process) that helped solidify a practice known as The Waterfall Method. The Waterfall Method means that each phase of a software development project is completed in turn and then it is handed off to the next set of workers.

The SDLC (Software Development Life Cycle) looked like the following:

1. Business Analysts -- examined manual processes that someone wanted to automate (turn into a computer program) and gathered requirements in formal documentation.
2. The Business Requirements would be handed to a Software Development team (Project Manager, Software Development Manager and Software developers) and they would guesstimate how long it would take to build the software. The guesstimate was _always_ wrong by some huge amount. Always.
3. The Software Development team would build software and complain about the requirements document not answering questions and would guess their way to a running product.
4. The Development Team would hand the software over to QA / Test (Quality Assurance) who would then break the software in every conceivable way.
5. Software developers and Development manager would fight with QA to "explain" why the software does actually meet the requirements and finally yell at QA telling them that they are "cotton-headed ninny muggins who didn't know nothing about software anyways and we are deploying this software with or without your sign-off."

6. Finally, the software (which was considered to be perfect since it met the Business Requirements and passed QA) was placed in production where customers would begin to use it.

7. Customers would call in to Customer Support and yell at them because the software didn't do what they originally wanted it to do. The Customer Support team would:
   a. Calm the customer down
   b. Explain to the customer why she is wrong
   c. Create workarounds to prove the customer is wrong
   d. Hang up and yell at the staplers on their desks about how stupid the software developers are who couldn't even make software that works the way the customer wants it to work.
   e. Have nervous breakdowns from constantly being so angry about the way the software works.
   f. Quit and open a chinchilla farm

8. The software would languish in production for years as customers accepted that it worked that way while creating workarounds to make it do the stuff they really wanted it to do in the first place (and hadn't those Business Analysts ask them all about this stuff in the first place?).

9. Finally, the old Development Manager would retire and a new one would take her place and say something like, "I think we should re-write the XYZ system. Let's get the Business Analysts to go and Gather Requirements for what the customers really want."

Notice that along the way, there is really no checking and fixing. Instead, each team of workers just does their thing and hands it to the next team who can only focus on the project from one angle -- from the viewpoint of their own role.

This is a waterfall method because it is preferable to throw yourself over a waterfall than it is to live your career in this type of way. No, no, no. It's really called the Waterfall Method because each time work is completed, it is as if the deliverable (Requirements doc, software, test results, etc) are just thrown over the waterfall to the next team. There is no real way to give feedback along the way. So instead of feedback, in those days, we just complained about the other teams.

Dev: "If QA would test right then my software would run fine!!"
QA: "If those devs weren't such idiots they could actually build software that passed tests."
Dev: "If those nincompoop Business Analysts could actually write up a valid Requirements doc we could probably build the right software."
Customer Support: "Ya'all are stupid and all the customers do is yell at us."
Business Analysts: "I tried to tell you what the customer wants but you people don't know what you're doing."

Here's how the problems were originally explained back in the 70s,80s,90s.

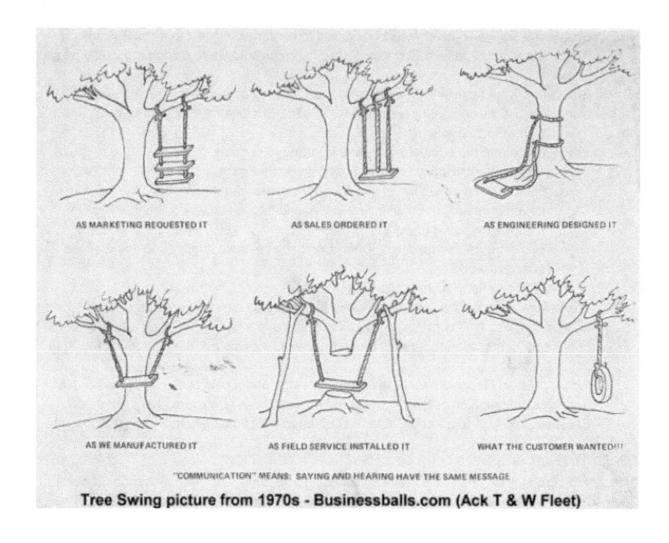

Tree Swing picture from 1970s - Businessballs.com (Ack T & W Fleet)

And the following Dilbert comic from January 29, 2006 explains exactly how difficult it is to get the requirements from the users: https://dilbert.com/strip/2006-01-29

And this one too: https://dilbert.com/2006-02-04

Here's yet another Dilbert that shows the lengths that workers will go to in order to evade having to tell you their requirements: https://dilbert.com/strip/2006-02-26

Along Came Agile

Then along came a new way of doing things. It's called the Iterative Methodology.
Iterative means looping.

1. Decide on one or more things that you want the software to do and make a quick list
    (backlog). Add new items as you think of them.

2. Take action - start building one of the things on the list.
3. Test the one thing you built.
4. Fix things that didn't quite work out right.
5. Loop back to number 1.

That's all you need. Now orient the entire team toward the software.

"Working software is the primary measure of progress."*

* From the original 12 Principles of the Agile Manifesto
(http://agilemanifesto.org/principles.html).

The ultimate goal of writing software is : **Creating a Functioning Product!**

There is no rivalry (less rivalry) between teams and the finger-pointing ("well, we did our part, we can't help that the software doesn't work!") begins to fade away.

The team will be measured by how well the software fits the Primary Stakeholders' needs.
The Primary Stakeholder is the person or people who will actually use the software.

Easiest Way To Get To The Software That The People Want

One of the easiest ways to get to the software that the people want is to begin stating what they want from their viewpoint.

Enter, Stage Right, User Stories

Instead of long requirements documents we can begin to create a work list (aka backlog in Agile) by stating what the user wants. We do so like the following:

- As a user, I want to be able to select any emoji so I can add it to a document I am writing.
- As a user, I want to be able to collect new emojis and add them into the program so I can use them later in documents I am writing.
- As a user, I want to be able to view my emojis in categories so I can find the one I want more easily.
- As a user I want a list of my recently used emojis so I can find the one I want to use more easily.
- As a user I want this program to run all the time on my desktop so I can easily copy an emoji and paste it into a document or post I am writing.

MVP (Minimum Viable Product)

That seems like enough for now. If we get those basic functional abilities into our program we'll have something that will at least be a MVP (Minimum Viable Product). A MVP just means that the software is basically usable and at least does a couple of minor things that the user would realistically want/need to do.

Now that we have a list of functional items we can target, we are ready to begin some design and coding.
Tomorrow we will begin adding the HTML, JavaScript and CSS which will start the construction of our Moji app.

Day 42

We are going to design our moji app. Design of an app results from tools (programming languages) we use to build it.
That's how it is in real life too.

For example if I am going to build something out of wood I need a totally different set of tools than if I'm going to build it out of Lego blocks. For the wood project, I'm going to need saws, drills, sanders, a work area, etc. However for the Lego project I'm basically going to need a clean space to work and all of the different shaped Lego pieces that the project will require.

Choosing Building Materials Sets Us Down A Path

Do you see how that choosing our building materials sets us down a specific development path? It is the same with software. If I tell you I'm going to build the app using C# then you are most likely going to use Visual Studio and build it using WPF (Windows Presentation Foundation). Visual Studio provides a way to view the WPF code that makes up the User Interface of the application. However, you are going to find that some things are possibly more difficult under this development framework. One of those will be deployment since WPF basically runs on Windows machines, it means that users will have to install the app on their machines.

Requirements Also Push Us In Design Directions

Some of the requirements may offer ideas about which development path may offer better choices too. One of the main reasons that software development has moved toward Web Apps is because deployment to all platforms (Windows, Linux, MacOS) is so much easier. Basically, you target the web browser and you can be confident it will run for the user no matter what Operating System (OS) they are running. However, if you choose to develop a desktop app you will have to choose a particular Operating System.

The Browser Is the Operating System

The Internet and web browsers have brought everything to everyone. It feels really painful to put a lot of work into developing an app and then having various users not be able to run it because it is not targeted to their OS.

This is one of the main reasons why this book focuses on Web Technologies: you can deploy your apps and get people to try them simply by pointing their web browser at your URL (Uniform Resource Locator -- web address).

Choosing a Particular Technology Is Also A Constraint

However, when you choose a particular technology you also accept that there are constraints within that technology. Not every development technology allows every functionality that you would like.

Copying to Clipboard

A great example of this is copying data to the user's clipboard so she can paste it. In an Android, iPhone, iPad or Windows desktop app this functionality works perfectly fine. However, on the web there are some challenges and it works a bit differently in various browsers on various platforms. iOS devices (iPhone, iPad) alter some of their web controls and cause some challenges that are solved easily if you are developing directly for the specific platform.

Our Chosen Limitation: HTML

We have made a decision to develop using HTML (browser-related technology) and we are stuck within those constraints. That leads us to an understanding that our User Interface is going to be built in HTML (even if we decide to use some Web Framework that wraps up HTML for us -- ReactJS, Angular, etc.).

Twitter Bootstrap User Interface

I happen to know that the Bootstrap CSS (Cascading StyleSheets) can provide us the visual elements and controls that will be extremely helpful to us in this project.

Toolkit Is Somewhat Arbitrary Decision

But, please keep this in mind: A Toolkit is an arbitrary decision made by the developer. Of course, developers often get very attached to their toolkits because anything we know is often far more desirable than anything we don't know. Many devs have spent years using one particular toolkit and they are convinced it is the greatest thing ever.

You Can Just Use Pure HTML and CSS

Also, keep in mind you can just use Pure HTML, CSS and hand-code everything. However, it will probably take you longer. That's the point of using (in this case) Twitter Bootstrap pre-made styles. Some really smart devs along with some really great graphic designers have created a set of re-usable HTML controls that will allow you to get to your finished product much quicker.

That means we should be able to attain our main goal which I will repeat here again:

"Working software is the primary measure of progress."

You Are Ready

Because of everything you've learned so far about HTML and CSS you will learn Twitter Bootstrap far more quickly and I believe you will be amazed by it.

Let's go.

Create the Main User Interface

We are now going to create the main User Interface. Bootstrap will allow us to do this extremely fast because there are some pre-built things we can use.

The main Bootstrap site is: https://getbootstrap.com/
There's a lot of documentation and information there.

Adding Bootstrap To Our Project

You can download bootstrap locally and then add links and script tags to the index.htm page so that it will reference the bootstrap library. However, there is a way that is a bit easier.
Bootstrap uses special CDN URLs (Content Delivery Network) to provide access to the library.

What are Benefits Of Using CDN?

There are quite a few benefits of using the CDNs.
1. They are very easy to add to your project. Just follow the steps to add them to your page(s).
2. You don't have to worry about downloading code and then making sure the bootstrap code is available on your web server and all that maintenance.
3. Your browser will cache the libraries that are retrieved via CDNs so if your user has already loaded a page that uses the same CDN the page may load from their cache and it is a lot faster.
4. The servers running on the CDN are basically available 100% of the time. No worries about outages etc. It's all handled by the CDN.

Add CSS CDN
First we add the CDN to the main Bootstrap styles (CSS).
If you go to the introduction page for Bootstrap you'll find the links we are using. By the time you read this they may be slightly altered since Bootstrap is continually doing updates.
https://getbootstrap.com/docs/5.0/getting-started/introduction/

You'll see something like the following:

Quick start

Looking to quickly add Bootstrap to your project? Use jsDelivr, a free open source CDN. Using a package manager or need to download the source files? Head to the downloads page.

CSS

Copy-paste the stylesheet `<link>` into your `<head>` before all other stylesheets to load our CSS.

```
<link href="https://cdn.jsdelivr.net/npm/bootstrap@5.0.0-beta2/dist/css/bootstrap.min.css"
```
Copy

JS

Many of our components require the use of JavaScript to function. Specifically, they require our own JavaScript plugins and Popper. Place **one of following** `<script>`s near the end of your pages, right before the closing `</body>` tag, to enable them.

Bundle

Include every Bootstrap JavaScript plugin and dependency with one of our two bundles. Both `bootstrap.bundle.js` and `bootstrap.bundle.min.js` include Popper for our tooltips and popovers. For more information about what's included in Bootstrap, please see our contents section.

```
<script src="https://cdn.jsdelivr.net/npm/bootstrap@5.0.0-beta2/dist/js/bootstrap.bundle.mi
```
Copy

You can just click the [Copy] button under the CSS heading.
Then paste it into our index.htm.

After that you'll want to grab the JavaScript link under the Bundle heading.

Here's what your newly updated index.htm will look like:

<!DOCTYPE html>
<html lang="en">

```
<head>
    <title>moji: manage your emojis</title>
    <meta charset="utf-8">
    <link href="https://cdn.jsdelivr.net/npm/bootstrap@5.0.0-
beta2/dist/css/bootstrap.min.css" rel="stylesheet" integrity="sha384-
BmbxuPwQa2lc/FVzBcNJ7UAyJxM6wuqlj61tLrc4wSX0szH/Ev+nYRRuWlolflfl"
crossorigin="anonymous">
    <script src="https://cdn.jsdelivr.net/npm/bootstrap@5.0.0-
beta2/dist/js/bootstrap.bundle.min.js" integrity="sha384-
b5kHyXgcpbZJO/tY9Ul7kGkf1S0CWuKcCD38l8YkeH8z8QjE0GmW1gYU5S9FOnJ0"
crossorigin="anonymous"></script>
</head>
<body>
    <h1>Moji</h1>
    <p>Manage your emojis!</p>
</body>
</html>
```

The CSS link and script lines are really long because they include some info to insure that the data coming back is the exact data you are expecting.

It insures that someone doesn't hack the CDN site and then attempt to deliver altered code that could affect you without you knowing.

Back to Git

Once you've made those changes, go ahead and check Git again.

The following snapshots are where I am running Git from my Linux (Ubuntu 20.04) terminal.

The messages are the same so you can see I ran :

$ git status

$ git diff

```
raddev@raddev-1:~/dev/moji$ git status
On branch main
Changes not staged for commit:
  (use "git add <file>..." to update what will be committed)
  (use "git restore <file>..." to discard changes in working directory)
        modified:   index.htm

no changes added to commit (use "git add" and/or "git commit -a")
raddev@raddev-1:~/dev/moji$ git diff
diff --git a/index.htm b/index.htm
index 598c57e..c3762c9 100644
--- a/index.htm
+++ b/index.htm
@@ -3,6 +3,8 @@
        <head>
                <title>moji: manage your emojis</title>
                <meta charset="utf-8">
+               <link href="https://cdn.jsdelivr.net/npm/bootstrap@5.0.0-beta2/d
ist/css/bootstrap.min.css" rel="stylesheet" integrity="sha384-BmbxuPwQa2lc/FVzBc
NJ7UAyJxM6wuqIj61tLrc4wSX0szH/Ev+nYRRuWlolflfl" crossorigin="anonymous">
+               <script src="https://cdn.jsdelivr.net/npm/bootstrap@5.0.0-beta2/
dist/js/bootstrap.bundle.min.js" integrity="sha384-b5kHyXgcpbZJO/tY9Ul7kGkf1S0CW
uKcCD38l8YkeH8z8QjE0GmW1gYU5S9FOnJ0" crossorigin="anonymous"></script>
        </head>
        <body>
                <h1>Moji</h1>
raddev@raddev-1:~/dev/moji$ █
```

Go ahead and commit the changes to continue tracking your changes.

$ git commit -a -m "Added CDN links to bootstrap resources."

Now, we're going to grab the main parts of our UI (User Interface) from a section of the Bootstrap web site that is categorized as Navs & Tabs. It's located on the menu (on the left side of the site) under the Components item.

You can get to the proper place using the following link:
https://getbootstrap.com/docs/5.0/components/navs-tabs/

You'll want to scroll down to the area that shows Vertical Pills.
This is a navigation interface that allows the user to click a button on the left which will load content on the right side.

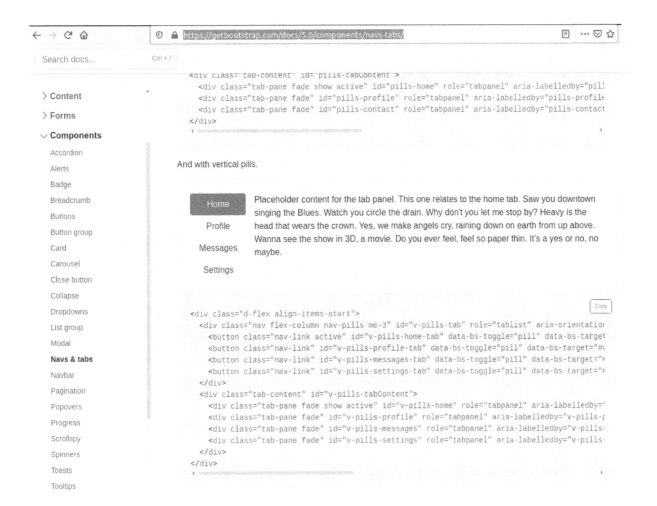

Once you get there click the [Copy] button over the code and we'll paste it into our page.

We'll go ahead and paste this over all of the currently existing body content. That means this will be the only thing between the opening and closing <body> tags.

Here's the updated index.htm.

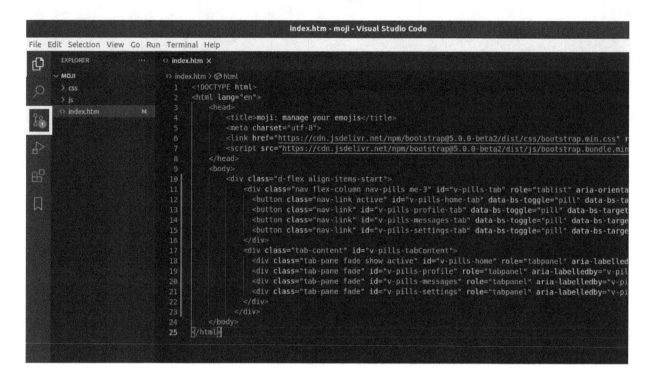

I like to show the code in case you are only reading along so you at least get an idea of what the code looks like. I haven't reproduced the actual HTML here (just the snapshot) because it's so much and it doesn't get formatted properly in the book. It's best to get the code from the GitHub repository (https://github.com/raddevus/LaunchYDC) and examine it in your editor.

Moji-2 From GitHub Repo

In case you are having any problem following along, you can just get the code found in the Moji-2 project and you will be up to date with these changes.

Source Control In VSC

In the previous image I highlighted the Source Control tab in Visual Studio Code.
Visual Studio Code hooks into the installed version control software (Git) and allows you some limited functionality.

Let's take a look.

Click on the Version Control tab so you can see a bit more.

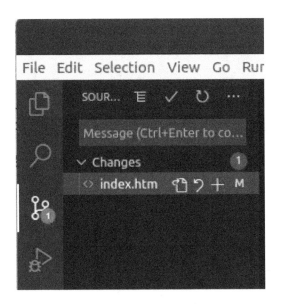

If you click the M (modified) it will display the changes that have been made to the file.

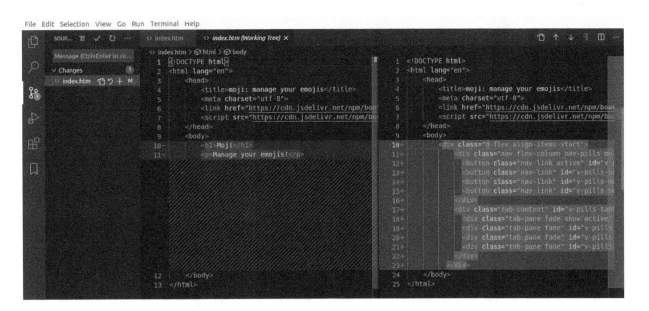

However, you cannot commit from here. You can stage the changes but we'll talk about that at a later time.

For now go ahead and check in your changes if you're following along. Or, again, you can get the code from the moji-2 directory of the Volume2 directory in the repo.

$ git commit -a -m "added basic nav layout which will be the main UI."

Now we can take a look at what we have so far.

You can navigate to the location where the index.htm file is in your file system and double-click it. When you do, you default web browser should load up the page.

Here it is running in FireFox on my machine.

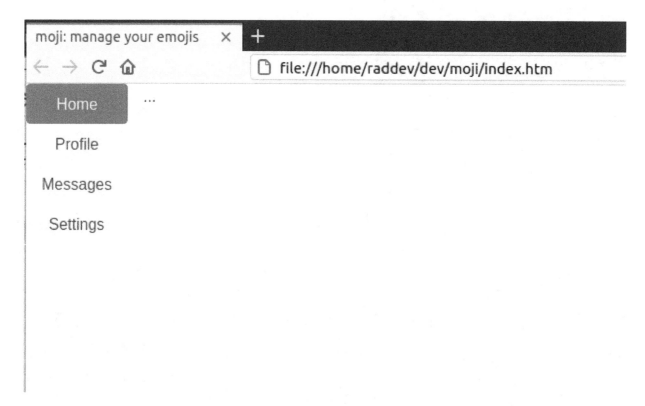

It doesn't look like a whole lot, but go ahead and click the nav buttons (aka pills) and you'll see that the content on the right loads. Well, the problem with the example we copied is that the content is the same on every one of the divs so you can't really tell we loaded a different div.

Tomorrow we are going to alter those divs so they will all have different content so you'll see that clicking each pill will show you something different.

This is a great start and we have learned a lot.
We've got Bootstrap loaded up and now we can take advantage of all the work that those great devs and graphic designers have already done for us.

Day 43

Yesterday's final example wasn't as fantastic as it could be because we stopped before showing different content when each of the buttons (pills) on the left were clicked. We are going to jump right in but I also want to show you how Git can be helpful if there is some time between your coding sessions. Git can remind you where you left off.

Git Helps You Remember

Run the following git command:
$ git log

```
commit 6be46e80467c579292a7a414627c0c404fd72619 (HEAD -> main)
Author: raddevus <1rade              ..com>
Date:   Mon Feb 15 18:13:19 2021 -0500

    added basic nav layout which will be the main UI.

commit 4b4c27f5aadf1c7d2bf1b84b6d722c54cfd32feb
Author: raddevus <1rade              ..com>
Date:   Mon Feb 15 17:36:53 2021 -0500

    Added CDN links to bootstrap resources.

commit 2bd7b854c4b6e482c4a70a327941bf0d78260512
Author: raddevus <1rade              .om>
Date:   Sun Feb 14 15:16:01 2021 -0500

    added initial html.

commit 6465f0c06237b85ce392f203d662fe991ea42129
Author: raddevus <1rade              .om>
Date:   Sun Feb 14 14:45:52 2021 -0500

    Adding initial files after repo creation.
raddev@raddev-1:~/dev/moji$ 
```

Good Commit Comments: Important!

Because of the git commit comments you have added you can get an idea of where you left off. That's why good comments are important. They are notes to your future self.

If you run $ git status right now you will not see anything because we checked in our code. However, there is a way to see the changes you last made.

You can run a diff between two revisions to see the last changes you made.

Git: List Files That Changed Between Two Revisions

First let's list the files that changed between two revisions. Since we are currently on revision : 6be46e80467c579292a7a414627c0c404fd72619

This is the revision number listed at the top of log listing (previous snapshot) which represents the current revision. Each time you commit a new revision number is created by git which it uses to identify the revision.

The previous revision number is : 4b4c27f5aadf1c7d2bf1b84b6d722c54cfd32feb

We will use that value to list the files that have changed since that revision.

Run the following command.
NOTE: You may have to use a different rev number if you've been following along and checking in then Git will create rev numbers that are on your computer.

$ git diff --name-status 4b4c27f5aadf1c7d2bf1b84b6d722c54cfd32feb

```
raddev@raddev-1:~/dev/moji$ git diff --name-status 4b4c27f5aadf1c7d2bf1b84b6d722
c54cfd32feb
M        index.htm
raddev@raddev-1:~/dev/moji$ █
```

You can see that it shows that index.htm was Modified.

Now, let's do a diff against that version to see the actual differences made in the file.

$ git diff 4b4c27f5aadf1c7d2bf1b84b6d722c54cfd32feb

```
diff --git a/index.htm b/index.htm
index c3762c9..54a8a4b 100644
--- a/index.htm
+++ b/index.htm
@@ -7,7 +7,19 @@
                <script src="https://cdn.jsdelivr.net/npm/bootstrap@5.0.0-beta2/
dist/js/bootstrap.bundle.min.js" integrity="sha384-b5kHyXgcpbZJO/tY9Ul7kGkf1S0CW
uKcCD38l8YkeH8z8QjE0GmW1gYU5S9FOnJ0" crossorigin="anonymous"></script>
        </head>
        <body>
-           <h1>Moji</h1>
-               <p>Manage your emojis!</p>
+           <div class="d-flex align-items-start">
+                   <div class="nav flex-column nav-pills me-3" id="v-pills-
tab" role="tablist" aria-orientation="vertical">
+                       <button class="nav-link active" id="v-pills-home-tab"
data-bs-toggle="pill" data-bs-target="#v-pills-home" type="button" role="tab" ar
ia-controls="v-pills-home" aria-selected="true">Home</button>
+                       <button class="nav-link" id="v-pills-profile-tab" data
-bs-toggle="pill" data-bs-target="#v-pills-profile" type="button" role="tab" ari
a-controls="v-pills-profile" aria-selected="false">Profile</buttona>
+                       <button class="nav-link" id="v-pills-messages-tab" dat
a-bs-toggle="pill" data-bs-target="#v-pills-messages" type="button" role="tab" a
:
```

We can now see that we added the HTML for the pills and divs that is our User Interface. This helps us remember where we left off.

More Than One Screen Full

Notice that the output is more than one screen full and there is more to list. This is indicated by the waiting flashing block cursor and the : (colon).

SpaceBar Advances Git Entire Screen

At this point you would either type q (to quit the listing) or press your space bar to see more.

Enter Advances Git One Line

You can also press <ENTER> to move the listing forward one line at a time.

When the listing is complete, you'll see the (END) block (see next image).

Q Key: Quits Git Listing

At this point you need to type q to quit out of the listing.

```
+                                <button class="nav-link" id="v-pills-settings-tab" dat
a-bs-toggle="pill" data-bs-target="#v-pills-settings" type="button" role="tab" a
ria-controls="v-pills-settings" aria-selected="false">Settings</button>
+                            </div>
+                        <div class="tab-content" id="v-pills-tabContent">
+                            <div class="tab-pane fade show active" id="v-pills-hom
e" role="tabpanel" aria-labelledby="v-pills-home-tab">...</div>
+                            <div class="tab-pane fade" id="v-pills-profile" role="
tabpanel" aria-labelledby="v-pills-profile-tab">...</div>
+                            <div class="tab-pane fade" id="v-pills-messages" role=
"tabpanel" aria-labelledby="v-pills-messages-tab">...</div>
+                            <div class="tab-pane fade" id="v-pills-settings" role=
"tabpanel" aria-labelledby="v-pills-settings-tab">...</div>
+                        </div>
+                </div>
        </body>
</html>
\ No newline at end of file
(END)
```

Make Changes For Better Example

Now, we have a good idea of where we left off, let's make our changes that will give us a better idea of what the pill navigation does for us.

Go back to Visual Studio Code and make sure you have your moji project folder open in VSC. Open up index.htm and take a look.

Right now we are focusing on all the HTML that is between the open and close body tags.

```
<body>
    <div class="d-flex align-items-start">
        <div class="nav flex-column nav-pills me-3" id="v-pills-tab" role="tablist" a
        <button class="nav-link active" id="v-pills-home-tab" data-bs-toggle="pill"
        <button class="nav-link" id="v-pills-profile-tab" data-bs-toggle="pill" dat
        <button class="nav-link" id="v-pills-messages-tab" data-bs-toggle="pill" da
        <button class="nav-link" id="v-pills-settings-tab" data-bs-toggle="pill" da
        </div>
        <div class="tab-content" id="v-pills-tabContent">
        <div class="tab-pane fade show active" id="v-pills-home" role="tabpanel" ar
        <div class="tab-pane fade" id="v-pills-profile" role="tabpanel" aria-labell
        <div class="tab-pane fade" id="v-pills-messages" role="tabpanel" aria-label
        <div class="tab-pane fade" id="v-pills-settings" role="tabpanel" aria-label
        </div>
    </div>
</body>
```

I've marked out two inner divs that we'll focus on.
  1. The first inner div contains the four buttons which are displayed on the left side of the User Interface.

2. The second inner div contains four more divs. Each of those four divs represent the content that is displayed when the button on the left is clicked.

Remember HTML Button Syntax

First of all notice that these are all simple HTML constructs. Bootstrap uses normal HTML which is supported by all the major browsers. Bootstrap just applies styles in a very special way so all elements are stylized in a uniform manner.

Here's a refresher of how you set up a simple HTML button.
<button>Button Display Text</button>

That will display in the browser something like the following:

Button Display Text

As you remember, the text that is displayed on the button is added between the opening and closing tags. The Bootstrap buttons are set up the same way. They just have the uniform styling applied over them (which comes from that original link to the CSS that we added at the top of index.htm).

Here's the HTML of the first button (labeled as Home):

```
<button class="nav-link active" id="v-pills-home-tab" data-bs-
target="#v-pills-home" type="button" role="tab" aria-controls="v-
pills-home" aria-selected="true">Home</button>
```

Numerous Attributes On the Button

There are numerous attributes on the Bootstrap button and it is those attributes that give it special styling and functionality.

Class Attribute

We've discussed the class attribute in Volume 1 you can see that the button has two values for the class attribute.
- Nav-link - provides styling to the button
- active - makes the button display as if it is selected (dark color)

When the page is initially loaded the [Home] button and selected and the active style makes it look as if it is selected.

The three other items do not have this value on their class attribute until they are clicked by the user.

Viewing Styles In Bootstrap StyleSheet

You can see the values in the Bootstrap stylesheet if you would like to examine them.

Point your browser at:
https://cdn.jsdelivr.net/npm/bootstrap@5.0.0-beta2/dist/css/bootstrap.css

This will load the stylesheet in your browser.

```
@charset "UTF-8";
/*!
 * Bootstrap v5.0.0-beta2 (https://getbootstrap.com/)
 * Copyright 2011-2021 The Bootstrap Authors
 * Copyright 2011-2021 Twitter, Inc.
 * Licensed under MIT (https://github.com/twbs/bootstrap/blob/main/LICENSE)
 */
:root {
  --bs-blue: #0d6efd;
  --bs-indigo: #6610f2;
  --bs-purple: #6f42c1;
  --bs-pink: #d63384;
  --bs-red: #dc3545;
  --bs-orange: #fd7e14;
  --bs-yellow: #ffc107;
  --bs-green: #198754;
  --bs-teal: #20c997;
  --bs-cyan: #0dcaf0;
  --bs-white: #fff;
  --bs-gray: #6c757d;
  --bs-gray-dark: #343a40;
  --bs-primary: #0d6efd;
  --bs-secondary: #6c757d;
  --bs-success: #198754;
  --bs-info: #0dcaf0;
  --bs-warning: #ffc107;
  --bs-danger: #dc3545;
  --bs-light: #f8f9fa;
  --bs-dark: #212529;
  --bs-font-sans-serif: system-ui, -apple-system, "Segoe UI", Roboto, "Helvetica Neue", Arial, "Noto Sans", "Liberation Sans",
UI Symbol", "Noto Color Emoji";
  --bs-font-monospace: SFMono-Regular, Menlo, Monaco, Consolas, "Liberation Mono", "Courier New", monospace;
  --bs-gradient: linear-gradient(180deg, rgba(255, 255, 255, 0.15), rgba(255, 255, 255, 0));
}

*,
*::before,
*::after {
  box-sizing: border-box;
}

@media (prefers-reduced-motion: no-preference) {
  :root {
    scroll-behavior: smooth;
  }
}

body {
  margin: 0;
  font-family: var(--bs-font-sans-serif);
  font-size: 1rem;
  font-weight: 400;
  line-height: 1.5;
  color: #212529;
  background-color: #fff;
```

Not Minified!

Notice that I sent you to the link that ends with the filename of bootstrap.css.
That is the non-minified file. Minification is a special process that removes as much of the whitespace as possible to reduce the file size and reduce the amount of data sent to the user.

We originally included the minified css file in our index.htm since it is smaller. That file is named bootstrap.min.css. This is a convention that you will see used often to indicate that the file has been minimized. Minimized files are not easy to look at though.

Here's the minified version. It's quite ugly.

Search For nav-link

Once you open the non-minified version, type CTRL-F in your browser (to begin a search in the text) and type nav-link so you can see what the original Bootstrap devs did to create the style for this class of items.

```css
.nav {
  display: flex;
  flex-wrap: wrap;
  padding-left: 0;
  margin-bottom: 0;
  list-style: none;
}

.nav-link {
  display: block;
  padding: 0.5rem 1rem;
  text-decoration: none;
  transition: color 0.15s ease-in-out, background-color 0.15s ease-in-out, border-color 0.15s ease-in-out;
}
@media (prefers-reduced-motion: reduce) {
  .nav-link {
    transition: none;
  }
}
.nav-link.disabled {
  color: #6c757d;
  pointer-events: none;
  cursor: default;
}

.nav-tabs {
  border-bottom: 1px solid #dee2e6;
}
.nav-tabs .nav-link {
  margin-bottom: -1px;
  background: none;
  border: 1px solid transparent;
  border-top-left-radius: 0.25rem;
  border-top-right-radius: 0.25rem;
}
.nav-tabs .nav-link:hover, .nav-tabs .nav-link:focus {
  border-color: #e9ecef #e9ecef #dee2e6;
  isolation: isolate;
}
.nav-tabs .nav-link.disabled {
  color: #6c757d;
  background-color: transparent;
  border-color: transparent;
}
.nav-tabs .nav-link.active,
.nav-tabs .nav-item.show .nav-link {
  color: #495057;
  background-color: #fff;
  border-color: #dee2e6 #dee2e6 #fff;
}
.nav-tabs .dropdown-menu {
  margin-top: -1px;
  border-top-left-radius: 0;
  border-top-right-radius: 0;
}
```

The first block (in orange) is the familiar class definition (.nav-link{}) that we learned about in Volume 1.

You can see that it is set as a display: block type (meaning it will cause a line break after it is displayed). There is some padding style added then some transition styling that is related to animation that is displayed when the button is clicked.

That's a lot of work that the Bootstrap devs and graphic designers have taken care of for us.

Creates Common Look & Feel

We can just apply these styles to our buttons and know that all of our buttons will have a common look and feel in our app. The look and feel creates the User Experience (UX).

ID Attribute

The id attribute that is in the sample is a bit long and we will change all of the button ids to match what we will use them for.

data-bs-toggle Attribute: Bootstrap Custom

The data-bs-toggle="pill" attribute is a custom bootstrap attribute (not found in HTML standard definitions). This item is used to add the button to the group of buttons which work together to be toggled -- so that only one of the buttons in the group can be clicked and selected to active at a time. If you remove this attribute from one of the buttons, you will see that the button no longer takes on the active styling when you click it. It will no longer be considered as one of the buttons in the selection group.

Attribute Names Provide Clues

The name of the attribute contains -bs- and the bs stands for Bootstrap, of course. This helps identify where various attributes may be coming from when you are looking at HTML so you can more easily find its definition. Various CSS libraries will use their own naming schemes to help you differentiate various styles.

Fourth Attribute: Target Div

But, for now we'll look more closely at the fourth attribute on the button: data-bs-target="#v-pills-home"

This item tells the button that its target is the div with the id of "v-pills-home".
If you look in the second set of inner divs you will see there is a div with that id.

I've highlighted it here.

```
<body>
    <div class="d-flex align-items-start">
        <div class="nav flex-column nav-pills me-3" id="v-pills-tab" role="tablist"
            <button class="nav-link active" id="v-pills-home-tab" data-bs-toggle="pil
            <button class="nav-link" id="v-pills-profile-tab" data-bs-toggle="pill" d
            <button class="nav-link" id="v-pills-messages-tab" data-bs-toggle="pill"
            <button class="nav-link" id="v-pills-settings-tab" data-bs-toggle="pill"
        </div>
        <div class="tab-content" id="v-pills-tabContent">
            <div class="tab-pane fade show active" id="v-pills-home" role="tabpanel"
            <div class="tab-pane fade" id="v-pills-profile" role="tabpanel" aria-labe
            <div class="tab-pane fade" id="v-pills-messages" role="tabpanel" aria-lab
            <div class="tab-pane fade" id="v-pills-settings" role="tabpanel" aria-lab
        </div>
    </div>
</body>
```

Each of the buttons has a data-bs-target that points to its associated div.

Alter Associated Div Content

Now that you know how each button points to its associated content, it is easy to update the content to show something that allows you to see the buttons in action.

Here's the current content of the home (just three dots (...) aka an ellipsis).

```
<div class="tab-pane fade show active" id="v-pills-home"
role="tabpanel" aria-labelledby="v-pills-home-tab">...</div>
```

Let's update the content right now so it tells us we are on the home item.

```
<div class="tab-pane fade show active" id="v-pills-home"
role="tabpanel" aria-labelledby="v-pills-home-tab">You are Home!</div>
```

Once you make that change and save it. You can reload the page.

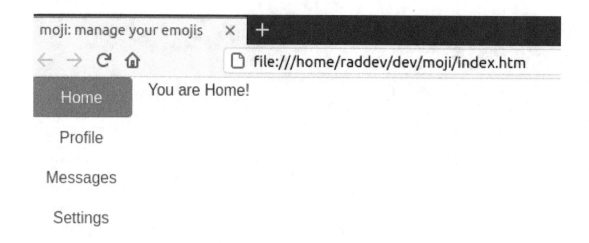

Now you can tell you are on the Home selection. Go ahead and click any of the other buttons and you'll see they still contain the ellipsis.

For our final work today let's go ahead and change the last three items so they all contain something different.

Here's the code.

```
<div class="tab-pane fade" id="v-pills-profile" role="tabpanel"    aria-labelledby="v-pills-profile-
tab">
    <image src="https://i.stack.imgur.com/3nKkw.png" width="550px">
</div>
<div class="tab-pane fade" id="v-pills-messages" role="tabpanel" aria-labelledby="v-pills-
messages-tab">
    <image src="https://i.stack.imgur.com/A9m9s.png" width="500px">
</div>
```

```
 <div class="tab-pane fade" id="v-pills-settings" role="tabpanel" aria-labelledby="v-pills-settings-
tab">
    <image src="https://i.stack.imgur.com/4t6NW.png" width="550px">
</div>
```

Hopefully you can tell that each of the divs now contain a different image.

Here's the first one you'll see when you click the [Profile] button.

GitHub : Volume2, moji-3

You can get the code by copying the moji-3 directory and taking a look at it.

You can also see this live at jsfiddle: https://jsfiddle.net/raddevus/c7wsuj24/13/
The code there is probably slightly different but you'll get the idea of how it all works.

Bootstrap Is Powerful

Consider how easy all of this is using the Bootstrap library. If we did all of this work ourselves
(styling the content, making the JavaScript that displays each panel, etc.) we would have spent
a lot of extra time to get it all to work and look right. This is how pre-made libraries can help us
get to a completed product far faster.

The Importance Of Understanding What Libraries Do

However, we never want to rest on just slapping things together. We always want to understand how things really work underneath it all so that when we get stuck we can figure out a workaround.

Tomorrow we'll do a few things:

1. Change the buttons so they have text that will make sense for our app.
2. Add different moji content for each panel (div area).

Day 44

The entire point of our moji app is to :

> Allow the user to easily select and copy one or more emojis so she can paste them into her target document.

The reason we are using the Pills / Panels User Interface is because we want to break the emojis into various groups so the user can find an emoji faster.

I suggest the the app be broken up into the following sections:

- Recent
- Faces
- Hands
- Animals
- Food
- Misc
- Custom

Let's clean up the existing code by making the IDs a bit shorter and then we'll also add pills for each of the categories I just listed.

Accessible Rich Internet Applications (ARIA)

As we move along you are going to see that there are numerous attributes on the Bootstrap controls which are marked as `aria-[name]` where the [name] portion is some specific verb or noun which attempts to describe the item. These are based upon a standard created by the W3C (more at https://www.w3.org/TR/wai-aria-1.1/) and are used to make websites more accessible to people who use assistive technologies to interact with web sites.

Here's a snapshot of all the changes that I made which include adding all of the categories above.

```
10   <div class="d-flex align-items-start">
11       <div class="nav flex-column nav-pills me-3" id="v-pills-tab" role="tablist" aria-orientation="vertical">
12           <button class="nav-link" id="recent-pill" data-bs-toggle="pill" data-bs-target="#recent-tab" type="button" r
13           <button class="nav-link active" id="faces-pill" data-bs-toggle="pill" data-bs-target="#faces-tab" type="butt
14           <button class="nav-link" id="hands-pill" data-bs-toggle="pill" data-bs-target="#hands-tab" type="button" rol
15           <button class="nav-link" id="animals-pill" data-bs-toggle="pill" data-bs-target="#animals-tab" type="button"
16           <button class="nav-link" id="food-pill" data-bs-toggle="pill" data-bs-target="#food-tab" type="button" role=
17           <button class="nav-link" id="misc-pill" data-bs-toggle="pill" data-bs-target="#misc-tab" type="button" role=
18           <button class="nav-link" id="custom-pill" data-bs-toggle="pill" data-bs-target="#custom-tab" type="button" r
19       </div>
20       <div class="tab-content" id="v-pills-tabContent">
21           <div class="tab-pane fade" id="recent-tab" role="tabpanel" aria-labelledby="recent-tab">You are Home!</div
22           <div class="tab-pane fade show active" id="faces-tab" role="tabpanel" aria-labelledby="faces-tab">
23               <image src="https://i.stack.imgur.com/3nKkw.png" width="550px">
24           </div>
25           <div class="tab-pane fade" id="hands-tab" role="tabpanel" aria-labelledby="hands-tab">
26               <image src="https://i.stack.imgur.com/A9m9s.png" width="500px">
27           </div>
28           <div class="tab-pane fade" id="animals-tab" role="tabpanel" aria-labelledby="animals-tab">
29               <image src="https://i.stack.imgur.com/4t6NW.png" width="550px">
30           </div>
31           <div class="tab-pane fade" id="food-tab" role="tabpanel" aria-labelledby="food-tab">food</div>
32           <div class="tab-pane fade" id="misc-tab" role="tabpanel" aria-labelledby="misc-tab">misc</div>
33           <div class="tab-pane fade" id="custom-tab" role="tabpanel" aria-labelledby="custom-tab">custom</div>
34       </div>
35   </div>
```

Get Moji-4

I've also added a one word piece of content to the new categories so you'll see "food" when you select the [food] pill, "misc" when you select the misc pill, etc.

This way you can see that the pill buttons are wired up and they actually work.

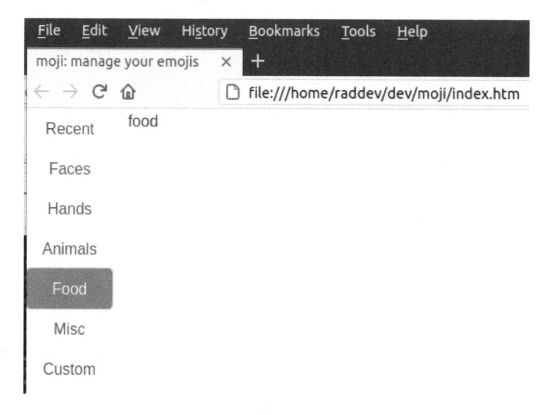

You can get the code from the /moji-4 directory from the GitHub volume2 resource.

Adding Some Emoji Faces

Let's add some emoji faces that will be a part of the faces-tab div.
We are going to add all of these as individual spans so there will not be any breaks between them and if the browser is resized they'll get wrapped in the div.

Finding Emojis

I went out to w3schools and found a nice list of emoji character codes.   Remember character codes? We talked about them in volume 1. You can read more about the basics of emojis as they are used in HTML at: https://www.w3schools.com/Html/html_emojis.asp

You can see a large list of emojis at : https://www.w3schools.com/charsets/ref_emoji.asp

Here's the first list of face emojis we'll add.

```
<span>&#128512;</span>
<span>&#128513;</span>
<span>&#128514;</span>
<span>&#128515;</span>
<span>&#128516;</span>
<span>&#128517;</span>
<span>&#128518;</span>
<span>&#128519;</span>
<span>&#128520;</span>
<span>&#128521;</span>
<span>&#128522;</span>
<span>&#128523;</span>
```

I'm using the decimal value so that each character entity is of the form:
$#NNN; where NNN represents the decimal value of the character.

You can see where I've added them to the faces-tab here.

```
20              <div class="tab-content" id="v-pills-tabContent">
21                  <div class="tab-pane fade" id="recent-tab" role="tabpanel" aria
22                  <div class="tab-pane fade show active" id="faces-tab" role="tab
23                      <span>&#128512;</span>
24                      <span>&#128513;</span>
25                      <span>&#128514;</span>
26                      <span>&#128515;</span>
27                      <span>&#128516;</span>
28                      <span>&#128517;</span>
29                      <span>&#128518;</span>
30                      <span>&#128519;</span>
31                      <span>&#128520;</span>
32                      <span>&#128521;</span>
33                      <span>&#128522;</span>
34                      <span>&#128523;</span>
35                  </div>
```

Now when you load the page you'll see some emoji faces.

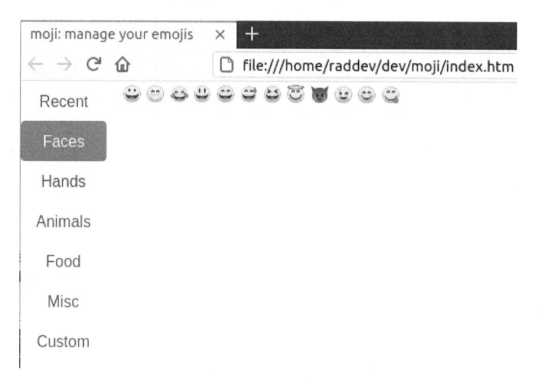

If you float over the faces in the tab area you will see that your cursor turns into an I-bar cursor (indicating that the web browser believes there are characters that can be selected or typed).

Let's change the I-bar cursor into a pointer hand using some CSS.

Go back to VSC and open up the /css/main.css (which is currently empty) and add the following code.

```
.emoji{font-size:x-large;
       background: whitesmoke;
       cursor:pointer;}
```

The new style will make the emojis appear a bit larger since we've added the font-size style and you'll see a very light grey background and of course the new hand pointer.

Go ahead and save the main.css file.

We are creating a CSS class selector for a class named emoji. Now let's add the emoji class to all of our tab divs.

I've added the emoji class to all of the tabs as the third class item. These tabs already have their class set to other values and we are just adding ours in. You can add the new class anywhere in the class definition for each element but I just made it the third one to keep them all in order.

Link In the main.css

We also need to link in the main.css file. Of course, we do this at the top of our index.htm in the head section. I make it the last <link> tag in the file so it is after the current <link> tag that pulls in the Bootstrap from the CDN.

```
<link href="css/main.css" rel="stylesheet">
```

```
<div class="tab-pane fade emoji" id="recent-tab" role
<div class="tab-pane fade emoji show active" id="face
    <span>&#128512;</span>
    <span>&#128513;</span>
    <span>&#128514;</span>
    <span>&#128515;</span>
    <span>&#128516;</span>
    <span>&#128517;</span>
    <span>&#128518;</span>
    <span>&#128519;</span>
    <span>&#128520;</span>
    <span>&#128521;</span>
    <span>&#128522;</span>
    <span>&#128523;</span>
</div>
<div class="tab-pane fade emoji" id="hands-tab" role=
        <image src="https://i.stack.imgur.com/A9m9s.png
</div>
<div class="tab-pane fade emoji" id="animals-tab" rol
        <image src="https://i.stack.imgur.com/4t6NW.png
</div>
<div class="tab-pane fade emoji" id="food-tab" role="
<div class="tab-pane fade emoji" id="misc-tab" role="
<div class="tab-pane fade emoji" id="custom-tab" role
```

Refresh CTRL-F5

Now, when we refresh, we'll see a different color background for the emojis and they'll be slightly larger (and easier to see).

Get into the habit of using CTRL-F5 when you refresh after making changes. This will force your browser to truly reload the index.htm and all the associated items (CSS, JS files, etc.). There are times when you'll make a change and the browser doesn't reload your changes properly and it can drive you crazy.

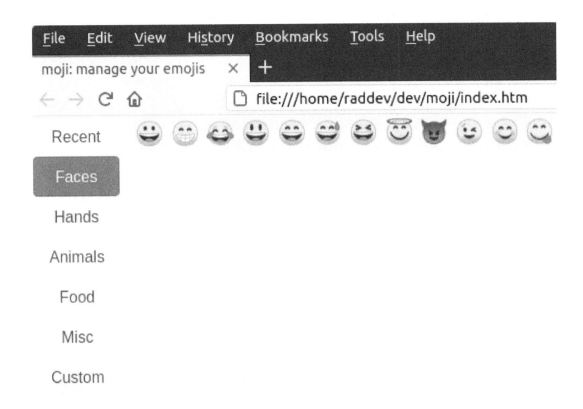

Get the Code - moji-5

Make sure you float over the emojis so you can see that the cursor also changes.
You can get the code from the GitHub repo in volume2\moji-5 folder.

Clicking Doesn't Select Emoji

You may notice that clicking an emoji doesn't select it. The entire idea of this app is that a user can click one or more emojis so she can copy them. Currently, you can select emojis but you cannot easily select more than one. And it is a bit too easy to accidentally select the space in between the emojis. You can double-click an emoji and it will be selected, but that's not great or obvious. There are just a few different things that occur that make it less than optimal the way it is.

JavaScript To Help Select Emojis

Let's write some code that will make it so that when the user simply clicks on an emoji then it will be selected. And, if the emoji is already selected then it will become unselected. This will allow the user to select multiple emojis even if they aren't next to each other.

Since we've done quite a bit of work today, we will jump in and start writing that code tomorrow.

Day 45

A LIttle Background On Emoji Character Sets

Note: Keep in mind that emojis are character codes which suggest what the emoji should look like. However, they are not represented the same way on every system (platform -- Android, Win10, Linux, MacOS, iPhone, etc.). Each of the systems have a character set that represents each emoji character code and in some cases may even not have a character which represents the character.

I'm mentioning this because I wrote Day 44 on my Ubuntu 20.04 Desktop and the emojis looked like the following:

However, now I'm writing this entry (Day 45) on my Win10 laptop and when I load our page they look like:

You can learn more about the differences by checking out the very nice emojipedia reference. Here's a snapshot of the entry for "Happy face" (the first one in our list).

From https://emojipedia.org/grinning-face/

Copy and Paste

Copy and paste this emoji. 😃   Copy

Also Known As
😃 Happy Face
😃 Smiley Face

Apple Name
😃 Grinning Face

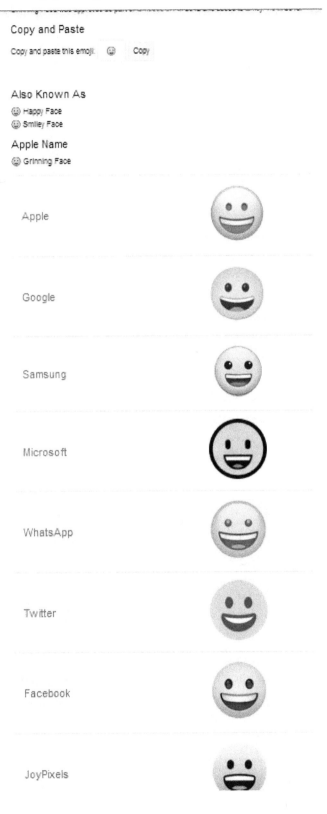

Apple	
Google	
Samsung	
Microsoft	
WhatsApp	
Twitter	
Facebook	
JoyPixels	

JavaScript Is Our Focus

Today we are going to be focusing on the JavaScript aspect of our little app because we want something to happen (select a character) when an event (click) occurs.

Most Direct Way, Not the Best

In this case we can add code in a direct way to make this happen. I'm going to show you this way first because you may see this type of code around. And, if we were only adding this code to one span or div it might be valid. However, in our case we need to add the click eventhandler to every span (every emoji) on our page and that would be a lot of repetitive code.

Add an onclick Event to Span HTML

You can simply add an onclick event to the Span HTML and attach it to a JavaScript function.

We'll go ahead and add the code to the first two emojis just so you can tell it works on any of the spans.

Here's the change we need to make in the HTML.
```
<span onclick="displayChar(this)">&#128512;</span>
<span onclick="displayChar(this)">&#128513;</span>
```

This code uses an HTML Event attribute (onclick) which will call a function (displayChar()) which we will write in our JavaScript. The function could've been named anything -- it is up to us to name it.

HTML Event Attributes: Pre-defined Names

Remember, these event attributes have pre-defined names and you have to match them to get them to work.
You can see a list of valid HTML Event Attributes at:
https://www.w3schools.com/tags/ref_eventattributes.asp

This registers the click event in the browser so it will watch and do something when the element is clicked with the mouse. If you don't register the event in some way then the click would just be ignored by the browser.

Event Handler : Getting the Terminology

We are responsible for writing the Event Handler (the JavaScript function which does something when the event occurs). We've named our event handler displayChar but we could've named it anything. You may see handlers named like spanClickHandler() in an effort to name them something that another developer may quickly recognize and understand what the function is used for.

What is that Word? : this

You may have also noticed that in our case we are passing a value into the function that is simply the word: this. this (all lowercase) is a special JavaScript keyword which is the way JavaScript refers to the current object. It's like an anonymous way to refer to the item that is calling the showChar() function. In our case this is the element that the user clicked. You see, the browser (and JavaScript) know the exact element you have clicked when you click it and this is the keyword we use to refer to the element object that is clicked.

We need the current element in our function so that we can use it to determine what character it contains (which emoji it contains).

The JavaScript handler code will make this a bit more evident. Add the following function definition to your js/main.js file.

```
function displayChar(element){
    alert(element.innerHTML);
}
```

That is the function definition so we name the incoming parameter element so we can remember what the incoming value represents. It represents the currently clicked span element. We know that because we added an onclick EventHandler to the span element.

Add Reference to js/main.js

We just need to add a reference that points to our js/main.js file into our index.htm so it knows to load the JavaScript so it will be available for use.
In this case we will load the JavaScript before the rest of the document so let's just add it at the top after the bootstrap JS file.

You can see it here:

```
<> index.htm  ✕      JS main.js          # main.css

<> index.htm > ⊗ html > ⊗ head > ⊗ script
   1    CTYPE html>
   2    l lang="en">
   3    <head>
   4        <title>moji: manage your emojis</title>
   5        <meta charset="utf-8">
   6        <link href="https://cdn.jsdelivr.net/npm/bootstrap@5.0.0-beta2/dist/
   7        <link href="css/main.css" rel="stylesheet">
   8        <script src="https://cdn.jsdelivr.net/npm/bootstrap@5.0.0-beta2/dist
   9        <script src="js/main.js"></script>
  10    </head>
  11    <body>
  12        <div class="d-flex align-items-start">
  13            <div class="nav flex-column nav-pills me-3" id="v-pills-tab" rol
  14                <button class="nav-link" id="recent-pill" data-bs-toggle="pill
```

Using the Script Tag

We simply use the HTML Script tag to include our JavaScript like the following:

```
<script src="js/main.js"></script>
```

As long as you get the path correct, all should work fine.

Let's refresh (CTRL-F5) or load the page in the browser and see what happens when we click the first or second emoji. Since we didn't add the onclick handler to any of the other spans, they will not fire our function.

What displayChar(this) Does

Our function gets the element clicked (incoming via the parameter to our function) and uses that element to examine the innerHTML property. The innerHTML property represents the text that is contained between the two span tags. Since our element only contains one character (the emoji) it then displays that character using the JavaScript alert() method.

Contrast to outerHTML Property

If we had called the outerHTML property on the element:

`element.outerHTML`

We would've seen the entire span HTML including the emoji character:

```
<span onclick=\"displayChar(this)\">□</span>
```

You Can Get the Code To Examine It

You can get the code and examine it in the moji-6 directory of volume2 of the GitHub repo.

Not Going to Keep This Code

This code helps us to learn about what is going on and how to create an event handler but it would be mostly problematic to add the event to every one of our spans which include an emoji. If we have hundreds of emojis we would have to include this on hundreds of the emoji spans and that is mostly annoying. There must be a better way.

There Is A Better Way

Of course there is! That's why we're talking about it right now.
Because programming is automation, we are going to automate the finding of all of the spans so we can add an event handler to each one of them. We'll do this with code instead of having to type in the event handler on each of the spans. This will also help us learn a few more JavaScript concepts.

A Hint To How We'll Do It

We'll do this work tomorrow but here is a hint. Remember when we used document.querySelector() to select one element? Do you also remember using the document.querySelectorAll() which would retrieve all elements that matched the selector? That's what we're going to look into tomorrow.

Day 46

Preparing For the Day's Work

To prepare for today's work, I did the following:
1. Deleted the displayChar() function definition from main.js since we don't need it. At this point main.js is empty again.
2. Removed the HTML DOM event handler onclick from each of the spans I had added it to in index.htm.

However, I left the <link> to the main.css and the <script> tag which references the main.js in index.htm.

Ready to Add Event Handlers

We are now ready to write our code which will add event handlers to all the spans in the document. To do that work we need to understand how to iterate through all of the spans found on the page. Fortunately, the document.querySelectorAll() method will help us do that.

To use the querySelectorAll() method we have to understand what type of object it returns.

querySelectorAll Information

We can take a look at the MDN (Mozilla Developer Network) documentation at :
https://developer.mozilla.org/en-US/docs/Web/API/Document/querySelectorAll

It explains that the return type is called a NodeList.

NodeList Provides Hierarchical Element Data

The NodeList is a collection of objects which are called Nodes. These Nodes are an abstraction of the HTML elements that they represent but provide some additional properties about the element which you wouldn't be able to determine from the HTML element itself. The additional properties of the Node object provide hierarchical information about the element such as:
- .nodeParent (returns the element that is the parent of the current item -- if it exists)
- .nodeChildren (yet another NodeList of all elements which are children of this node)
- .nodeName (this is different for various elements but most often returns the type of element (span, div, etc.)

There are many other properties which can help you traverse the hierarchy of nodes in your HTML document. Since HTML is basically a tree structure with a root element (body) and any numbers of leaves (all inner elements) which can in turn contain other leaves the NodeList and Nodes provide a way to iterate through the hierarchical tree that the HTML creates.

At point we don't need to understand everything about the NodeList because we just want to be able to attach an EventListener to each span node.

How We'll Select Our Span Nodes

In an effort to only select the correct spans we are going to use a Selector that uses two parts. We are going to select the spans which are inside a div which has the emoji class (which we earlier defined).

We are working with what we have in the HTML.

Specifically the part shown here:

```
<div class="tab-pane fade emoji show active" id="faces-tab"
role="tabpanel" aria-labelledby="faces-tab">
    <span>&#128512;</span>
    <span>&#128513;</span>
    <span>&#128514;</span>
```

```
<div class="tab-pane fade emoji show active" id="faces-tab"
    <span>&#128512;</span>
    <span>&#128513;</span>
    <span>&#128514;</span>
    <span>&#128515;</span>
    <span>&#128516;</span>
    <span>&#128517;</span>
```

Our call to document.querySelectorAll will look like the following:

```
document.querySelectorAll(".emoji span");
```

Insures Only Emoji Spans Are Selected

This will insure that only the spans which are nested inside of an element which has the emoji class set will be selected. That way if we add a span somewhere else in the document which is not related to the emoji then it will never be selected.

What we want to do now is iterate over every Node in the collection that is returned from querySelectorAll() and add the EventListener to the element (represented by the Node).

I'm going to show you two ways to iterate over these. First, the older way, and then the newer way which is a bit cleaner and shorter code.

First Way : For Loop

Here's the code which I've commented to explain what happens.

```
function attachEmojiClickListeners(){
    console.log("in attachEmojiClickListeners...");
    // First get the collection of Nodes that we want to work with
    // and store the collection in a variable for later use
    let allNodes = document.querySelectorAll(".emoji span");

    // Next, use a for loop to iterate over each Node in the collection
    // The NodeList provides a property named length to determine
    // how many nodes are in the list and we use that now.
    for (let i = 0; i < allNodes.length; i++){
        allNodes[i].addEventListener("click", function() {
        alert(allNodes[i].innerHTML);
        }); // end of addEventListener function
    } // end of For loop
} // end of function
```

Here's a snapshot that may be easier to read.

```
JS main.js        ● ⟨⟩ index.htm        # main.css

js > JS main.js > ⬡ attachEmojiClickListeners
  1
  2    function attachEmojiClickListeners(){
  3        console.log("in attachEmojiClickListeners...");
  4        // First get the collection of Nodes that we want to work with
  5        // and store the collection in a variable for later use
  6        let allNodes = document.querySelectorAll(".emoji span");
  7
  8        // Next, use a for loop to iterate over each Node in the collection
  9        // The NodeList provides a property named length to determine
 10        // how many nodes are in the list and we use that now.
 11        for (let i = 0; i < allNodes.length; i++){
 12            allNodes[i].addEventListener("click", function() {
 13                alert(allNodes[i].innerHTML);
 14            }); // end of addEventListener function
 15        } // end of For loop
 16    } // end of function
 17
```

There are a few things to get accustomed to in this code. When you first see it, it can be a bit ugly because of the anonymous function that we pass into the addEventListener() function can be a bit confusing since it has those extra braces inside the the parameter list.

Keep in mind that addEventListener takes two parameters:
1. The name of the event it will listen for (as a string) -- "click" in our case
2. A function which will run when the event occurs.
   a. Remember you can pass in the function itself and if it is defined elsewhere then you just pass the name (not wrapped in double-quote)
   b. You can also pass an anonymous function that you define on the fly -- that is what we did in this example. We passed a function that has only one line of code (the alert() call

Get Code: Try It Now

Get this version of the code from the moji-7 folder and load it up in your browser.

It Actually Won't Quite Work

When you do, you'll find that clicking an emoji doesn't actually do anything (yet).

Function Definition Doesn't Run Until Called

That's because even though we defined the attachEmojiClickListeners() function, it has not been called. Keep in mind that a function definition doesn't run until it is called. And, in our case the function is never called.

First, Let's Call the Function Manually

However, I want to show you how to call the function from the web browser's developer console.

Here are the steps.
1. Make sure you have the code from moji-7 directory ready to run.
2. Double-click the index.htm file (to open it in your default browser).
3. From your browser press the F12 button (which should open your developer console). Make sure you open the console tab so it has focus. We are going to run some code. It'll look like the image below.

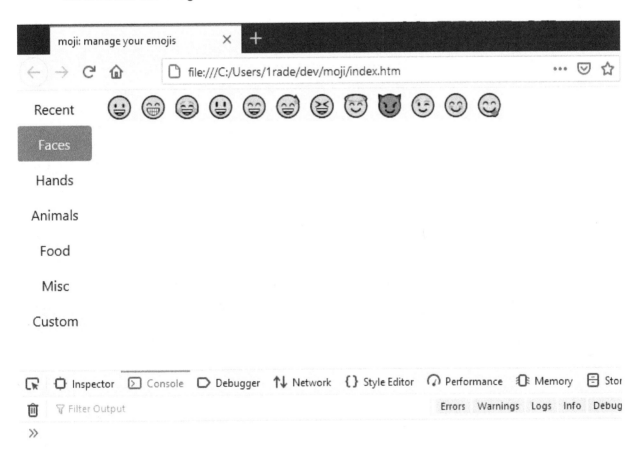

4. Run the following (which is a call to the method we created).

a. >> attachEmojiClickListeners()

Once press <ENTER> and the function runs it will look something like the following snapshot.

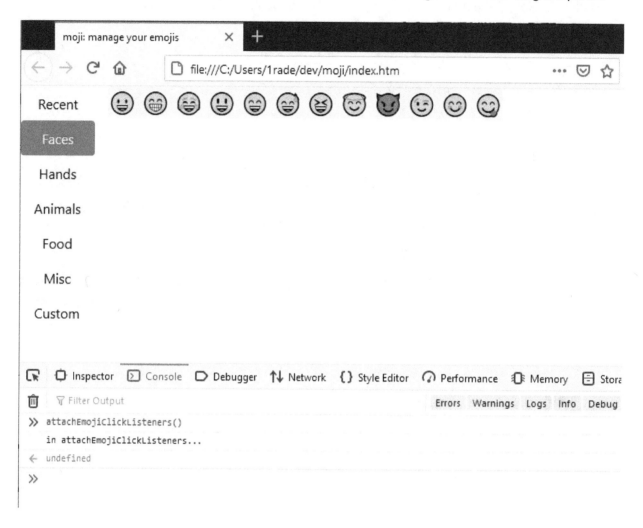

As you can see, the method ran and the console.log("in attachEmojiClickListeners...") -- the first line in the function -- ran and output the message so you know that the function did actually run.

Now, you can click any one of the emojis and it will now run the alert() code that will display the specific emoji that the user clicks.

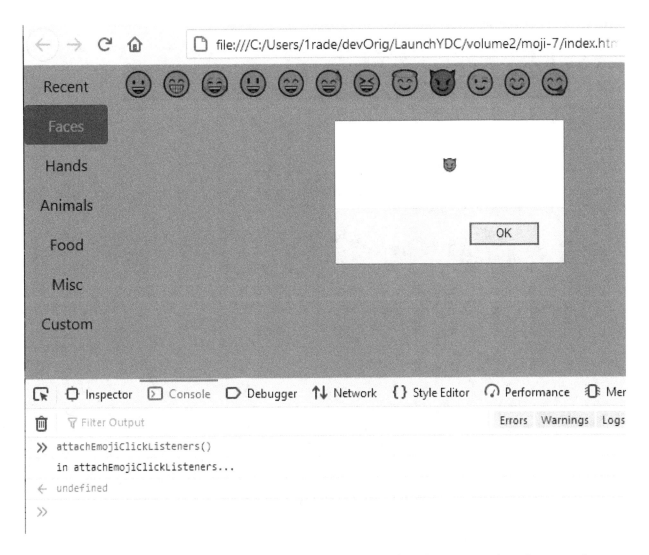

But this isn't quite correct, of course, because we want the function to run when the page is completely loaded. That's where another EventListener / EventHandler comes into play.

Onload Event

We need to make sure the web page automatically runs the attachEmojiClickListeners() function each time it is loaded. To do that we could add the onload event handler to the HTML like the following:

`<body onload="attachEmojiClickListeners()">`

However, we want to add our EventListener in our JavaScript. It's very simple to do. We just add the following line of code to the top of main.js.

`addEventListener("load",attachEmojiClickListeners);`
Now the entire main.js will look like the following:

```
JS main.js    ✕    <> index.htm    # main.css

js > JS main.js > ...
   1 │   addEventListener("load",attachEmojiClickListeners);|
   2
   3     function attachEmojiClickListeners(){
   4         console.log("in attachEmojiClickListeners...");
   5         // First get the collection of Nodes that we want to work with
   6         // and store the collection in a variable for later use
   7         let allNodes = document.querySelectorAll(".emoji span");
   8
   9         // Next, use a for loop to iterate over each Node in the collection
  10         // The NodeList provides a property named length to determine
  11         // how many nodes are in the list and we use that now.
  12         for (let i = 0; i < allNodes.length; i++){
  13             allNodes[i].addEventListener("click", function() {
  14                 alert(allNodes[i].innerHTML);
  15             }); // end of addEventListener function
  16         } // end of For loop
  17     } // end of function
  18
```

Reload the page (CTRL-F5) in your browser and now clicking the emoji will work without manually calling the function and if you look in the console you'll see the output line that tells you that the function did already run.

Moji-8 Has Updated Code

You can get the current version in the moji-8 folder of the volume2 folder in the GitHub repo.

About For Loops and Collections

Let's talk about how the for loop works and a little more about the Nodes collection.
The for loop is a special control structure which allows the same code to be run numerous times for each item in an array or list.

We have to do somet work to set up the for loop because a for loop expects special statements at the top which help it know when it should start and how long it should run for.

A for loop takes on the following type of structure where the semicolons separate each part of the loop header.

```
for ( [loop counter initialization] ; [boolean test for continue] ; counter increment / decrement)
{ // for loop body where work will be done }
```

Indexing Through A Collection

In our case we initialize a new variable to the value of 0. We do this because we are going to use the i variable as the indexer in the Nodes list. Collections in JavaScript (Lists, Arrays, etc) are referenced by an index value and their first item starts at index 0.

Boolean Test For Continue

The second part of the for loop is the test so the for loop can know when it should stop. We are telling the for loop to continue as long as the value of i is less than the value of the length of the collection. That means we will run the body of the for loop once for each item in the collection.

Infinite Loops Can Occur

As long as the boolean test returns true then the for loop will continue.
This can lead to infinite loops if the test never gets to a false value so beware.

Counter Increment / Decrement

Finally, the last part of the for loop is a place to increment the counter variable.
In our case we make this i++ which is the same as i = i + 1; It simply increments the value of i by one each time at the end of the loop.

Increment / Decrement Runs After Body

This portion of the for loop runs after the body of the loop runs. This is important to understand so you understand when the loop will end.

Inside the Loop Body

Inside the loop body (between the opening and closing curly brackets { }) is the code that we want to run a specific number of times.

We also use the i variable to index into the Nodes collection so we can reference the specific item we want to use.
We actually use the i variable to index the item in two places, but here is the first (when we add the eventlistener:

```
allNodes[i].addEventListener...
```

I haven't reproduced the entire line here because right now I want to focus on the allNodes collection.

allNodes is the collection of all of the Nodes that are represented by emoji spans.
But we want to reference each item inside that list, one at a time.
The way we do this is using the square bracket syntax.

allNodes.length gives us a property of the collection
But to reference a specific item, we use the square brackets and a valid index value
For example to get the name of the first item in the Nodes collection we could use:
allNodes[0].name

In our case, we are simply using a value that continually changes through the for loop so we can refer to each item in the list as we iterate over it.

allItems[i].addEventListener...

This allows us to attach the event listener to a specific item and not the collection. We want our event listener attached to each individual span that is contained in the Node list and this is how we do it.

That's it for today. Tomorrow we'll show you the updated way to insure all of the emoji spans get the event handler added and you'll learn how the newer code works.

Day 47

Numerous Ways To Do Same Thing

One of the challenges of learning to develop software is that at times there are numerous ways to do the same thing and when you begin learning you don't know which is the most correct or best way.

This is similar to the idea that just because something is working doesn't mean it is right. An example in the physical world could be using wires in an electronics project that are not thick enough for the amount of current that is being used. The device may work for a while until the wires overheat and melt, but the device isn't actually made properly or up to safety standards.

The Emotional Challenges of Software Development

As a new developer this will often lead to two different situations:
1. Believing the way you got something working is the best way because you got it working
2. Always wondering if the thing you got working isn't quite right.

These two opposite ideas lead many developers to two different types of self belief:
1. Believing you are a genius who writes code exactly the right way -- while thinking others who criticize it are dumb.
2. Impostor syndrome -- always thinking you are just barely hanging on and believing that soon your lack of knowledge will be found out and exposed

Transparency & Vulnerability

The reality is obviously somewhere in the middle of these two situations and displays the need for transparency. Transparency means communicating what your code does and how it works and being open to constructive criticism while ignoring abusive criticism.

Of course, transparency requires the ability to be vulnerable and many work-places are run by bullies or have bullies as lead devs or dev managers and they don't understand this need.

Continuing Education

This is why, if you choose the software development path you are accepting that your life will be a journey on the road of continuous education. I think this is a great thing. It's what keeps the job / career fulfilling and always exciting but you will have to decide if you feel that way.

Trade-offs Are Natural

The entire idea of trade-offs is a natural thing when creating something. It's like that engineering joke:

You can have any 2 of the 3:
1. Fast completion
2. Great quality
3. Low cost

However, you can't have all three because to get the other two you have to sacrifice the one. It's just the laws of physics. It's the constraints we work under in this world.

If you want Fast completion and Great quality you are going to have a pay for a fantastic and experienced team and it is going to cost you.

If you want it to be Fast completion and Low cost then don't expect great quality because we don't have time to test it or make it look beautiful.

Changes In Programming Languages

Changes in our tools and programming languages over time also cause things to change for us. So code that was fine in the past is now considered outdated.

In the past, before ECMAScript* 2015 (aka as ES6) was released we had to use the for loop shown in the previous code.

*ECMAScript is the official name of JavaScript which is standardized by Ecma International. You can see more at: https://en.wikipedia.org/wiki/ECMAScript

Whenever you see ESX (where X is a number) or ECMAScript just understand that they are talking about different versions of the JavaScript standard.

Even after the release of the new features it still takes a while for the browser to implement the functionality so even though 2015 sounds like a while ago now, it really isn't because these features came to the browsers and JavaScript developers a bit later.

Browsers and JavaScript Change

The next step for JavaScript came around 2009 with release 5 (ES5) but it was a quiet release and didn't have numerous new features. Also, not all browsers took up the new features so if you wanted to use the new features you had to be aware that not all browsers implemented them and you had to provide a workaround for those browsers. It wasn't great and it is why if you look at older HTML / JavaScript you may see a lot of extras and wonder why the devs add all of that extra code and even complain about it.

Replacing the For...Loop

There was one very interesting feature that came about in ES5 (2009-2010) but again not all browsers implemented it so even during this time many devs just ignored it because you couldn't expect all browsers to use the code anyways. This encouraged many devs to just keep using the original for loop type of structure.

What's So Bad About Regular For Loop?

There's not that much that is bad about the for loop, but keep in mind that often when you attempt to use one you are attempting to iterate over a collection.

Iterating Over A Collection

To iterate over the collection you need to start at the 0th index (first item) of the collection and continue until you are at the last item of the collection (collection length - 1).

Generally this means when you create a for loop you have to do three main things:
1. create a loop counter
2. Check to see if you are at the end of the collection
3. Increment the loop counter (if you're still not at the end of the collection)

That's what our loop did in the previous code.

```
for (let i = 0; i < allNodes.length; i++)
```

All the Extra Work

See all of that extra work?
We had to create the i variable just so we can use it to count the items in the collection.
Next, each time through the loop we had to check to see if the counter (i) was still less than the length of the collection. Finally, we also had to increment the counter so that the next time through the loop we would be using the new value as the index.

New(er) forEach Control Structure

The JavaScript developers took a look at this and thought,
1. We know how many items are in the collection
2. We know the user just wants to iterate over each item and do something with it

Why not create a new way that:
1. Iterates over every item in the list
2. Calls a user-provided function each iteration, which includes the current item

They added the forEach structure that allows us to change our for loop so it is much simpler.

First , take a look at our updated code that uses the forEach (notice that it no longer requires the loop counter variable) and then we'll talk about what it does in detail.

```js
JS main.js    X    <> index.htm        # main.css

js > JS main.js > ...
 1   addEventListener("load",attachEmojiClickListeners);
 2
 3   function attachEmojiClickListeners(){
 4       console.log("in attachEmojiClickListeners...");
 5       // First get the collection of Nodes that we want to work with
 6       // and store the collection in a variable for later use
 7       let allNodes = document.querySelectorAll(".emoji span");
 8
 9       // Next, use a forEach() to iterate over each Node in the collection
10       allNodes.forEach( function (node){
11           node.addEventListener("click", function() {
12               alert(node.innerHTML);
13           }) // end of addEventListener function
14       }); // end of forEachFunction
15   } // end of function
16
```

I'll use the line numbers from the code snapshot to reference each line we are talking about.

The forEach() function takes a function as a parameter and the function itself takes one parameter which represents the current element in the collection.

Anonymous forEach() Function

I'm going to unwrap the function that is wrapped up in the forEach() function call so you can see it a little clearer. These functions that take a full function can be a bit confusing to see when you are first learning about them.

```
function (node){
    node.addEventListener("click", function() {
      alert(node.innerHTML);
    }) // end of addEventListener function
} // end of anonymous function we are passing in to forEach()
```

In our example, that function is simply wrapped in the opening and closing ( ) parenthesis formed by the call to forEach().

Node Variable Name Can Be Anything

Also, the parameter named node can be named anything you like (as long as it is a valid variable name). That is just a placeholder that the forEach will use to reference the node item that it is passing in to the function each time it iterates over the NodeList.

That name is also the one we use to refer to the item inside the anonymous function. You can see that we changed :
```
allNodes[i].innerHTML
```
to
```
node.innerHTML
```

The Result: Shorter Code

The code does the same thing as our previous code, but is a bit shorter and doesn't require you to create the extra loop counter variable or evaluate to see if you are at the end of the list.
In this case we can concentrate on doing our work (attaching event handlers) and not worry about doing all that extra work to handle loop counters and determine if we are at the end of the collection.

That's a big step in your learning of JavaScript, flow control structures and the history of how these came about. However, ES6 provided quite a few more collection control structures and we will see how to use one named Map() tomorrow which will make things a bit cleaner again. We will also begin looking at Arrow functions which make using anonymous functions sent in as parameters a bit cleaner.

Get the Code : moji-9

You can get the code changes for the work we did today in the Volume2\moji-9 folder.

Day 48

Arrow Functions: Shorthand For Anonymous Functions

Let's talk about a new change to the JavaScript language called an Arrow function.
It is a shorthand for defining anonymous functions.

Let's get a refresher again on function definitions.

First there is the normal function definition:

```
function [name](0 - many params separated by commas){
        // body of function
}
```

A quick example is:

```
function add(firstNumber, secondNumber){
    return firstNumber + secondNumber;
}
```

Now, let's create an anonymous function. We might do this because we need to pass the function into another function as we did in our forEach() example yesterday.

As an example, let's assume we have an array of values that we want to use, but we need to add 5 to every one of the items in the array.

Here's our array (list of values):
```
let allValues = [1,3,5,7,9];
```

```
const secondNumber = 5;
// now we use the forEach() structure to add the second number to every one of the values in the list. I'll store the values in a string and then later write them to a div so you can examine them.
let outputValues = "";
allValues.forEach (function (item){
    outputValues += item + secondNumber + ",";
});
document.querySelector("div").innerHTML = outputValues;
```

I've created a JS Fiddle so you can see this in action: https://jsfiddle.net/raddevus/91qxmeau/2/

You can see that each item has the value of 5 added to it.

```
HTML ▼
    1    <!DOCTYPE html>
    2  ▼ <html>
    3  ▼ <head>
    4      <meta charset="utf-8">
    5      <meta name="viewport" content="width=device-width">
    6  ▼   <title>JS Bin</title>
    7    </head>
    8  ▼ <body>
    9      <div></div>
   10    </body>
   11    </html>
```

```
CSS ▼
```

```
JavaScript + No-Library (pure JS) ▼
    1    let allValues = [1,3,5,7,9];
    2
    3    const secondNumber = 5;
    4    // now we use the forEach() structure to add the second number t
         o every one of the values in the list. I'll store the values in
         a string and then later write them to a div.
    5    let outputValues = "";
    6  ▼ allValues.forEach (function (item){
    7      outputValues += item + secondNumber + ",";
    8    });
    9    document.querySelector("div").innerHTML = outputValues;
```

6,8,10,12,14,

The point here is that the creation of the anonymous function is a bit ugly.

JavaScript Devs Trying To Make Syntax Cleaner

Again the JavaScript developers took a look at how a function is passed into a function and they noticed that they could make it a bit smaller.

They noticed that the function keyword was basically unnecessary so they removed it.

They decided that a function definition for an anonymous function could look like the following:

param => body

A param is sent into a body and the body of the function runs.

Let's alter our previous code so it uses the Arrow function.

allValues.forEach (item => outputValues += item + secondNumber + ",");

Now you can see that the anonymous function is just the one parameter coming into the function and the one line of the body.

This makes it a bit easier to see where the closing parenthesis is for the forEach() function and it makes it all a bit easier to read. However, it looks really odd if you don't know about Arrow functions.

I saved the code and you should be able to see it at this jsfiddle link:
https://jsfiddle.net/raddevus/91qxmeau/5/

So far that is really cool but there is a lot more to Arrow functions in JavaScript.

A lot of JS Devs are completely infatuated with Arrow functions so you are going to see them everywhere now. And they really do clean up a lot of code but if you aren't accustomed to recognizing them they can be very odd. You just need experience seeing them a bit. That's why we're going to alter our code to use them too.

The ES6 Map() Function

But before we begin to alter our code in our moji app, let's take a look at another structure which was added in ES6 that basically replaces the forEach() function.

We'll take our previous sample code and alter it and I'll save it as a jsfiddle version again.

for/of Loop Control Structure

We are now using the for/of structure.

In this case we alter the code to look like:

```
for (let item of allValues){
    outputValues += item + secondNumber + ",";
}
```
See the altered code at: https://jsfiddle.net/raddevus/91qxmeau/9/

```
1    let allValues = [1,3,5,7,9];
2
3    const secondNumber = 5;
4    // now we use the forEach() structure to add the second number t
     o every one of the values in the list.  I'll store the values in
     a string and then later write them to a div.
5    let outputValues = "";
6  ▾ for (let item of allValues){
7        outputValues += item + secondNumber + ",";
8    }
9    document.querySelector("div").innerHTML = outputValues;
```

This is simply the structure that recognizes that allValues is a collection (an Array) and that it can iterate over those items.

We have to create the new variable using let so that the variable is set to the value of each item as the loop is iterated over, but that is all we have to do. The code runs just as it previously did, but again the code is quite a bit more obvious and is again a bit shorter.

Less Code, Less Maintenance

Less code means less maintenance in the future. That is always good.

Let's Use for/of In Emoji

Now that we know about the for/of structure we can use it in our original emoji code.

Here's our very simple updated code using the for/of structure.

```
// Next, use a for/of to iterate over each Node in the collection
for (let node of allNodes){
   node.addEventListener("click", function() {
   alert(node.innerHTML);
   }) // end of addEventListener function
} // end of for/of
```

```
JS main.js    X    <> index.htm    # main.css

js > JS main.js > ...
  1    addEventListener("load",attachEmojiClickListeners);
  2
  3    function attachEmojiClickListeners(){
  4        console.log("in attachEmojiClickListeners...");
  5        // First get the collection of Nodes that we want to work with
  6        // and store the collection in a variable for later use
  7        let allNodes = document.querySelectorAll(".emoji span");
  8
  9        // Next, use a for/of to iterate over each Node in the collection
 10        for (let node of allNodes){
 11            node.addEventListener("click", function() {
 12                alert(node.innerHTML);
 13            }) // end of addEventListener function
 14        } // end of for/of
 15    } // end of function
 16    
```

See how much simpler the code is to read now that we don't need the anonymous function in there any more? It's a lot cleaner because the code we want to run is now listed right in the for/of body.

Now that you understand these new structures like the for/of and Arrow functions it will be far easier for you to learn other collection methods that were added to such as map(), reduce() etc. We will talk about those in upcoming lessons.

List of New Functionality From ES5 (2009) & ES6 (2015)

Here's a great resource at w3schools that is a list of the new functionality that ES5 & ES6 brought
- https://www.w3schools.com/Js/js_es5.asp
- https://www.w3schools.com/Js/js_es6.asp

Get The Code In moji-10

You can get the changes we made to the moji project in the volume2/moji-10 directory. This will include the change to the for/of loop.

That's all for today. Tomorrow we will begin to implement the real code that will do the select on the emojis and we'll remove the test code that simply uses alert(). We will also add some emojis to the other panels.

Day 49

Back on Day 41 we made a backlog (work list) that provides us with some guidance toward the final product we are attempting to create. Let's take a look at that backlog again to insure we are staying on track.

BackLog (WorkList)

- As a user, I want to be able to select any emoji so I can add it to a document I am writing.
- As a user, I want to be able to collect new emojis and add them into the program so I can use them later in documents I am writing.
- As a user, I want to be able to view my emojis in categories so I can find the one I want more easily.
- As a user I want a list of my recently used emojis so I can find the one I want to use more easily.
- As a user I want this program to run all the time on my desktop so I can easily copy an emoji and paste it into a document or post I am writing.

We are working our way through that first item but you will see that we are also creating code that will help solve the second item in the list.

As Software Developers we should always re-center ourselves on the targets we are attempting to hit so that we:

1. Only write code for the specific things that should be included in the project.
2. Make notes when we discover other needed functionality that arises as we develop the main BackLog. These items can then be fed back to the Product Owner and explained why they need to be added to support the overall project.

Dog-Fooding: Eat Your Own Dog-food

We should also be using the product and thinking like a user as we go. This is called Eating Your Own Dogfood (https://en.wikipedia.org/wiki/Eating_your_own_dog_food). It means that you are willing and excited to use the product that you are creating.

Steve Jobs & The Original iPod

Steve Jobs originally wanted a music device that was easy to use, held hundreds of songs and was no larger than a pack of cigarettes. This was the original iPod product and he was a user of the product. He was guiding others to build the thing he wanted and eating his own dog food.

Getting Users Involved

That's one of the reasons the iPod was so successful: there was a strong target user who was involved in the creation process.

As you work for companies and produce software, you will find that companies have great difficulty involving the end-users in the process. It is vastly important. Software projects fail over 50% of the time and the real reason is because the end-users don't want the product as it works or they can't tell what the product really does.

That's because too many technical people tried to create something that they themselves didn't want to use. They just created a product for some audience who they believed existed.

MVP : Minimum Viable Product

This is why we try to get a MVP (Minimum Viable Product) in front of real users as soon as possible. This way we can give them a little functionality (that doesn't overwhelm them) that they can try as early as possible. But it can still be quite difficult to get users involved. They don't really want to look at the thing until it does something that they want it to do. Hopefully, your MVP will have one feature that solves a problem for them. If it does, they'll use it.

Always Dog-Food

However, you should always be dog-fooding your work. You have to fall in love with the stuff you're building and start using it like a user. Be honest and gripe at yourself about the places where the app is difficult to use or confusing. Look at your app with fresh eyes and not just as the owner-dev that you are.

The Emoji App Was Something I Wanted

This emoji app was something I wanted because I would find myself on web sites attempting to post on a forum and I wouldn't have a way to easily add an emoji. I don't want the app to waste my time searching for an emoji I've already used. I don't want the thing to be difficult to use so I designed it to be as simple as possible. I also decided to use HTML, JS, CSS to create it because I wanted to be able to create it fast and access it from anywhere.

Let's jump back into the code. We'll try to complete all of the following today:
1. Add all initial emojis -- all emojis that will be a part of the project (grouped onto each tab area)
2. Make sure the click highlights each emoji and adds it to an array (list) of selected items which can all be copied.

The first thing we want to do is:

1. Remove the alert() code.
2. Replace it with the code which will run when an emoji is clicked.

Keep Code Clean: A Function Does One Thing

To keep your code clean, you want to break it up into manageable functions: functions that are as few lines of code as possible. This will make it easier to see what your code is doing later on when you go to fix a bug or add enhancements.

For our code, I"m going to replace the one line alert() call with a call to another function that we are going to create.

```
for (let node of allNodes){
    node.addEventListener("click", function() {
        handleEmojiClick(node);
    }) // end of addEventListener function
} // end of for/of
```

```
4    function attachEmojiClickListeners(){
5        console.log("in attachEmojiClickListeners...");
6        // First get the collection of Nodes that we want to work with
7        // and store the collection in a variable for later use
8        let allNodes = document.querySelectorAll(".emoji span");
9
10       // Next, use a for/of to iterate over each Node in the collection
11       for (let node of allNodes){
12           node.addEventListener("click", function() {
13               handleEmojiClick(node);
14           }) // end of addEventListener function
15       } // end of for/of
16   } // end of function
```

handleEmojiClick Function

The handleEmojiClick function will do the work that will occur when the user actually clicks an emoji. We want the work that it does to simply be :
1. Update the item on screen so it "looks selected".
2. Add the element to an array so we know which ones are selected.

But, wait, there's a bit more.
If the emoji is clicked a second time (clicked when it was already clicked) then we assume the user is unselecting the item and we want to remove the selection from the array and make it "look unselected".

Keeping Functions Simple & Readable

To keep our function as simple and readable as possible, I will further breakdown what the function does into other function calls.

Here's the code for handleEmojiClick():

```
function handleEmojiClick(el) {
    if (isSelected(el)){
        removeElement(el);
    }
    else{
        allSelectedElements.push(el);
    }
    displaySelectedElements();
}
```

```
18    function handleEmojiClick(el) {
19        if (isSelected(el)){
20            removeElement(el);
21        }
22        else{
23            allSelectedElements.push(el);
24        }
25        displaySelectedElements();
26    }
```

See how you can read this code almost as if it is regular English?
If el is selected then removeElement el.
Else (if el is not selected) then add (push) el to the allSelctedElements array.
Then, in both cases, displaySelectedElements(), which insures that the selected items are displayed as selected and other items are not.

allSelectedElements Array

Since we are using the allSelectedElements in a few different places we have made the array global so that each function is working on the same copy of the list of selected elements.
We've made it globally accessible to our script by defining it at the top of our main.js outside of any other function.

Global Variable

This array will be "registered" / instantiated by the browser when the main.js file loads into memory and will be available while the program runs (while the page is loaded in a browser window).

You can see the variable declaration at the top of the main.js before any other function is defined.
You can also see that it is up there with our addEventListener which we wanted to run when main.js is loaded.

```
JS main.js        ●      <> index.htm          # main.css

js > JS main.js > ⊗ handleEmojiClick
  1      addEventListener("load",attachEmojiClickListeners);
  2│     let allSelectedElements = [];
  3
  4      function attachEmojiClickListeners(){
  5          console.log("in attachEmojiClickListeners...");
  6          // First get the collection of Nodes that we want to
```

Now that we have a few more functions that run when handleEmojiClick() is fired, let's take a look at the functions that support that function.

Here is the list of functions that handleEmojiClick() calls:
1. isSelected(el)
2. removeElement(el)
3. allSelectedElements.push(el) -- push() is a JS provided function that allows you to add an element to an array.
4. displaySelectedElements()

isSelected : Determine If Element Is Selected

Notice that our if statement directly calls the isSelected() function. That is because we are returning a boolean value that tells the if statement if the item is selected or not.


```
function isSelected(el){
    let retVal = false;
    allSelectedElements.forEach(a => {
      if (a === el){
        retVal = true;
```

```
    }
  });
  return retVal;
}
```

```
39 ∨    function isSelected(el){
40           let retVal = false;
41 ∨         allSelectedElements.forEach(a => {
42 ∨             if (a === el){
43                     retVal = true;
44             }
45         });
46         return retVal;
47    }
```

This function uses a forEach() Array function that implements an Arrow function.

The forEach simply passes each item of the array (which is an HTML element) into the Arrow function : I've named each item as the letter a.

Inside the Arrow function, is a single if statement that compares the a element to the el element which is passed into the isSelected() function.

If any one of the items in the allSelectedElements array matches the el element (element passed into the function) then we know that the element has already been selected (and added to the allSelectedElements array. If the forEach() finds a matching element then it sets the return value (retVal) to true.

However, if forEach() never matches any of the items in the allSelectedElements then the item is not selected and the retVal stays false.

Finally, after the comparison is done, the function always returns the value of retVal (true or false).

This wraps up all of this code that does the comparison and moves all of these lines of code into this separate function so that you don't have to read all of these lines in the calling function. That makes it a lot more simple to read the code.

Back in our calling function, handleEmojiClick(), if isSelected returns true then a function is called to remove the element from the array: removeElement(el).

removeElement(el) : Remove Item From Array

I'm going to show you some older code which will iterate through the items of the array, find the one to remove and then remove it. You will likely come upon code like this so it will be good for you to learn what it looks like.

However, keep in mind that there are often numerous ways to get to the same solution. And, you may see a better way. If you do, I highly suggest you get the code and alter it to the better method. There is no better way to learn how to code.

```
function removeElement(el){
  let  foundItemIdx = 0;
  for (let i = 0;i < allSelectedElements.length;i++){
   if (allSelectedElements[i] === el){
       foundItemIdx = i;
       break;
    }
  }
  allSelectedElements.splice(foundItemIdx,1);
}
```

```
28      function removeElement(el){
29        let  foundItemIdx = 0;
30        for (let i = 0;i < allSelectedElements.length;i++){
31          if (allSelectedElements[i] === el){
32            foundItemIdx = i;
33            break;
34          }
35        }
36        allSelectedElements.splice(foundItemIdx,1);
37      }
```

We are going to use another JS provided Array method named splice() to remove a single item from our array of elements.

Array Splice() Function

The splice() method takes two parameters:
1. Index of the item to begin removing from the array
2. Count of number of items to remove from the array.

Since arrays are Zero-based in JavaScript, the smallest valid value the index can ever be is zero.

That's why we go ahead and initialize our foundItemIdx = -1. That indicates that we have found no value that matches and we don't want to remove any from the array.

Next, we set up the for loop so we can simply iterate through allSelectedItems and determine if any of them match the element which is passed into our function.
If any do, then we'll get the index value of the item in the array.
Finally, if there was a match we call the splice() method on the index and remove 1 element which removes just that one item from the array.

This handles the situation when the user clicks on an emoji that has already been selected (it removes it from the array..

Back up in the calling method, handleEmojiClick() we also handle the event when the user selects an unselected emoji.

Add Item To Array: Push()

We simply add the emoji to the array (allSelectedItems) using the JavaScript provided push() method.

```
18    function handleEmojiClick(el) {
19        if (isSelected(el)){
20            removeElement(el);
21        }
22        else{
23            allSelectedElements.push(el);
24        }
25        displaySelectedElements();
26    }
```

That is done inside the else{} portion of our code. .push() simply adds the element to the end of the array (pushing it onto the array).

displaySelectedElements()

Finally, after our array has the correct selected items only, we call displaySelectedElements() to insure that only the emojis that were selected look selected.

```
49    function displaySelectedElements() {
50        allSelectedElements.forEach(el => {
51            var range = document.createRange();
52            range.selectNodeContents(el);
53            var sel = window.getSelection();
54            sel.addRange(range);
55        });
56    }
```

We use some of the JavaScript provided DOM (Document Object Model) functions to do this work.

We want to iterate through the elements of allSelectedElements array so we use the forEach() again. Each time we use the element (el) that is passed to us from the array.

We call document.createRange() to create a selection range of characters.
We then set the range.selectedNodeContents() to the element.
Finally we get a selection from the JavaScript window object and then call addRange() with the range which contains all of our selected elements in it and they will display as selected.

Each time you click an emoji in our app all of this code fires.

Here's what it looks like when you select the 2, 4 and 5 items.

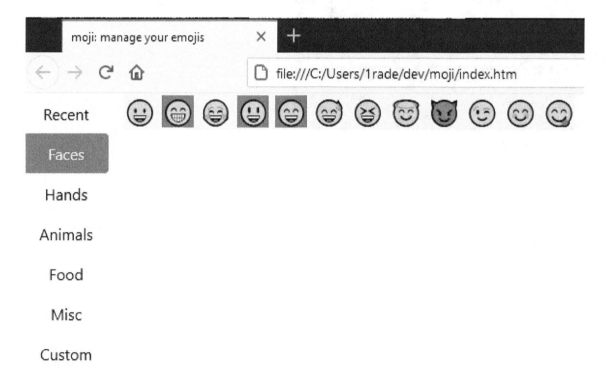

Now you can see that those items are selected. **Note**: Your highlight color (mine is blue) may appear different since it is dependent upon System settings and colors.

Also, if you press F12 and open the developer tools in your browser you can type the name of our array and see that three items are chosen.

```
 ▸   ☐ Inspector   ≫ Console   ◻ Debugger   ↑↓ Net

 🗑      ▽ Filter Output

     in attachEmojiClickListeners...

 ≫  allSelectedElements
 ←  Array(3) [ span, span, span ]
```

Get The Code : Volume2\moji-11

You can get the source in Volume2\moji-11 directory and try it out.
When you do, you'll see that you can select and unselect each of the emojis.

Copy & Paste Works

Now you can also select the emojis and then use CTRL-C to copy them. Afterwards you can paste them into any document using CTRL-V.

A Challenge / Issue

You will also find that it is a bit annoying that after you select a number of them, copy and paste them, then you have to manually unselect them one at a time (or refresh the page) to unselect them. We will add a button that unselects all of them in a future lesson.

Completing The MVP

Let's add all the base emojis into each tab now and that will create a really solid MVP (Minimum Viable Product) which will at least allow you to copy / paste a large number of emojis and begin using the app and discovering what else might need to be added.

I went ahead and add all the base emojis. Here's what the HTML looks like now for the faces tab.

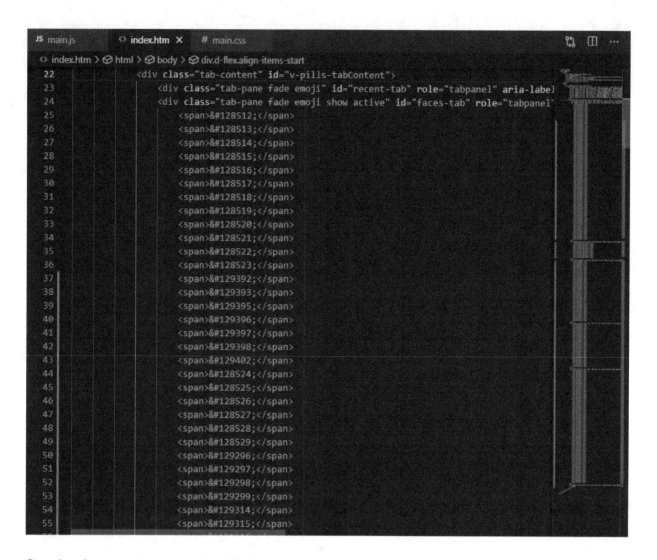

```
JS main.js        <> index.htm ✕      # main.css                                            ⟲  ▢  ···

<> index.htm > ⊘ html > ⊘ body > ⊘ div.d-flex.align-items-start
  22              <div class="tab-content" id="v-pills-tabContent">
  23                  <div class="tab-pane fade emoji" id="recent-tab" role="tabpanel" aria-label
  24                  <div class="tab-pane fade emoji show active" id="faces-tab" role="tabpanel"
  25                      <span>&#128512;</span>
  26                      <span>&#128513;</span>
  27                      <span>&#128514;</span>
  28                      <span>&#128515;</span>
  29                      <span>&#128516;</span>
  30                      <span>&#128517;</span>
  31                      <span>&#128518;</span>
  32                      <span>&#128519;</span>
  33                      <span>&#128520;</span>
  34                      <span>&#128521;</span>
  35                      <span>&#128522;</span>
  36                      <span>&#128523;</span>
  37                      <span>&#129392;</span>
  38                      <span>&#129393;</span>
  39                      <span>&#129395;</span>
  40                      <span>&#129396;</span>
  41                      <span>&#129397;</span>
  42                      <span>&#129398;</span>
  43                      <span>&#129402;</span>
  44                      <span>&#128524;</span>
  45                      <span>&#128525;</span>
  46                      <span>&#128526;</span>
  47                      <span>&#128527;</span>
  48                      <span>&#128528;</span>
  49                      <span>&#128529;</span>
  50                      <span>&#129296;</span>
  51                      <span>&#129297;</span>
  52                      <span>&#129298;</span>
  53                      <span>&#129299;</span>
  54                      <span>&#129314;</span>
  55                      <span>&#129315;</span>
```

See the document map on the right that shows a mini-view of the entire HTML? You can see that there is a lot of content that goes on for a long while. Those are all of the spans that contain the individual emojis.

All the Code Still Works!

That part is not very exciting but what is exciting is the fact that since we created the automated way of adding the addEventListener we don't have to do anything else but emoji click simply works as it did before we added all these additional emojis.

Here's a snapshot of the miscellaneous tab with a few items selected.

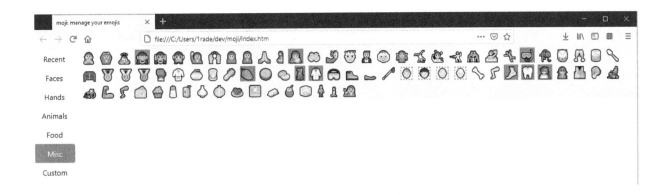

Too Wide and No Padding

I think the view is too wide and takes up too much width. It also makes the user have to move her cursor more left and right to select items. Also, do you see how the emojis are tight against the top? It doesn't look very nice.

We can fix both of these problems with a simple addition to the CSS, so let's do that right now.

Here's the fully updated main.css.

```css
.emoji{font-size:x-large;
    background: whitesmoke;
    cursor:pointer;
    max-width:600px;
    padding: 5px;
}
```

I added a max-width to the emoji class. It's an arbitrary value that I picked that insures the emojis will wrap to the next line and be more vertically oriented than horizontally.

I also added a padding of 5px to the emoji class so that there will be 5 pixels of distance between the emoji div and any other div. It just makes things look a bit better.

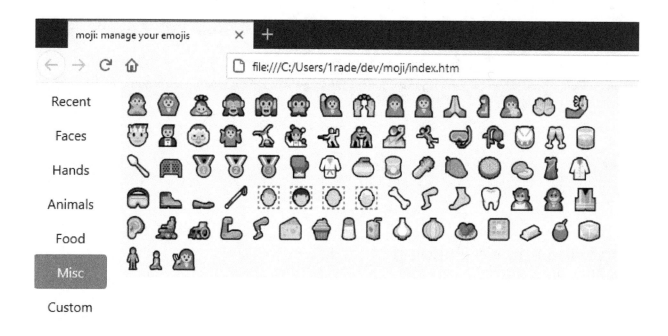

That's all the work for today -- and it was a lot.

Now you have a true MVP and you could begin using it now. But you'll find as you use it that there are some other nice features that we can add to make it more usable.

Get The Code : volume2\moji-12

Get the code and check it out. I think you'll like it and we've fulfilled our first user story of :

- As a user, I want to be able to select any emoji so I can add it to a document I am writing.

Discovered Small Bug

I also discovered a slight bug that occurs when you switch away from the page and come back or the focus gets taken away from the emoji div then the selected items don't show up properly. That is something that is easy to fix and we'll do it soon.

Day 50

First thing today, let's fix our bug.

To fix it, first we need to recreate the bug and understand what is happening.

Recreate the Bug

1. Select a few face emojis (see first image below)
2. Click anywhere in the whitespace of the page. Anywhere that there isn't an emoji. See second image below. Or you can click up in the nav bar (where you type the URL) -- Just make sure you don't refresh the page.

Step one, select some emojis.

Step two, click in the whitespace...I've placed some red dots in the next image, to show you where you can click.

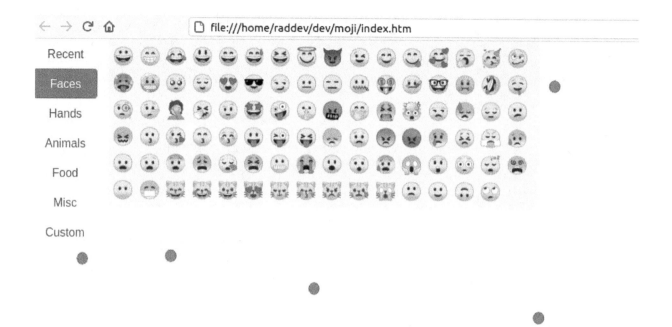

When you click in the whitespace of the document you will see that it no longer looks like any of your emojis are selected.

That's because the browser redraws the page and removes the selected items.

The items are still selected in your array though. It's just that we need to insure that no matter where the user clicks that the selection is redrawn every time.

Prove the Emojis Are Still Selected

You can prove that the items are still selected by:

1. Clicking any emoji. When you do, your list will be re-displayed. That's because clicking an emoji fires the code that adds or subtracts the clicked emoji and then runs the highlighting code.
2. Open up Dev Tools (F12) in your browser and take a look at the allSelectedElements array (See next image and you can see that 9 of my emojis are selected).

```
    in attachEmojiClickListeners...
>> allSelectedElements|
←  Array(9) [ span, span, span, span, span, span, span, span, span ]
```

HTML Document Object Model

Keep in mind that when you click anywhere in a web page you are activating some portion of the DOM. At the highest level you are at least clicking within the <HTML></HTML> tags.

That's important for us to know, because what we want to do to solve this problem is add an EventListener to the HTML tag so that if the user clicks anywhere then the code which will insure the correct emojis are selected is shown.

It's quite simple to add this code.

It's just one line of code that needs to run when main.js loads.

We are going to :
1. select on the HTML element.
2. Call addEventListener to register the handler
3. Set the event we want to listen to as "click"
4. Add an arrow function that calls the function that we already created: displaySelectedElements()

```
// this selector makes it so currently selected emojis are not unselected.
document.querySelector("html").addEventListener("click",
()=>displaySelectedElements());
```

Here's the code near the top of the file.

```
# main.css        JS main.js    ×    <> index.htm
js > JS main.js > ⊙ attachEmojiClickListeners > ⊙ node.addEventListener("click") callback
1     addEventListener("load",attachEmojiClickListeners);
2     let allSelectedElements = [];
3
4     // this selector makes it so currently selected emojis are not unselected.
5     document.querySelector("html").addEventListener("click", ()=>displaySelectedElements());
6
7     function attachEmojiClickListeners(){
8         console.log("in attachEmojiClickListeners...");
9         // First get the collection of Nodes that we want to work with
10        // and store the collection in a variable for later use
11        let allNodes = document.querySelectorAll(".emoji span");
12
13        // Next, use a for/of to iterate over each Node in the collection
14        for (let node of allNodes){
15            node.addEventListener("click", function() {
16                handleEmojiClick(node);
17            }) // end of addEventListener function
18        } // end of for/of
19    } // end of function
20
```

A List of Things You Had to Know Already

Think about how easy that fix was. But the reason it was so easy is because you already understand a lot of concepts. If you hadn't then it would've take a long time to teach you those first.

Here's the list of things you must understand:
1. Where code needs to be added to a JavaScript file so that it will run automatically when the JS file loads.
2. How to use document.querySelector()
3. What the HTML element is
4. What the DOM (Document Object Model) is
5. How to add event listeners and how they work
6. Arrow functions

It's a lot of things but all of it came together to help us figure out a solution.

Now when you select one or more emojis, they will always stay highlighted no matter where you click around. Another nice feature is that if you select another tab and then come back to the Faces tab you will see that they are still selected.

Get the Code and Try It Out: volume2/moji-13

The code is in the volume2/moji-13 folder so load it up in your browser and check out how it works now.

What About Mobile Browsers?

This seems like a good day for fixing bugs so let's take a look at what happens when you load our emoji app in a mobile browser.

Since you are view the page from the file system (double-clicking the file manager and having it display in your default browser) you will not be able to load it on a mobile device that is separate from your computer.

How might you view the page as if it were loaded by a mobile browser? Most of the web browsers provide a way to do this using the built in developer tools.

I'm running FireFox 86.0 (64-bit)

In FireFox (Google Chrome will be similar) you can :
1) Load our emoji app from the file system
2) open up dev tools (F12)
3) You'll see a small mobile icon somewhere, which will force the browser into Responsive Design mode (see next image).

○ Inspector ☐ Console ☐ Debugger ↑↓ Network {} Style Editor ⌒ Performance ◑ Memory ☰ Storage ✝ Accessibility 𐄷 Application

⎚ ▽ Filter Output   Errors Warnings Logs Info Debug   CSS   Responsive Design M

in attachEmojiClickListeners...   main.js:8:13

»

What Is Responsive Design?

Responsive Design just means making sure your web page resizes an behaves appropriately no matter which platform (Win10, Linux, Android, iPhone, etc.) the user is running when she loads your web page.

Right now when you click the Responsive Design button and choose one of the smaller width mobile devices (like the iPhone X/XS iOS 12) you will see that all the emojis look extremely small.

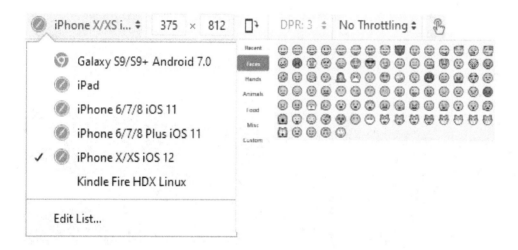

That will make it almost impossible for a user to select a specific emoji because they are using their finger and each touchpoint will most likely be larger than on emoji.

Fortunately this is very easy to fix, by simply adding a new meta tag to our HTML.

We simply need to set a meta attribute that is named viewport.
The viewport attribute allows us to set the initial width and scale that the user will see the web page sized to.

The following is the basic meta tag we will add to set the viewport to let the browser know that we want the content set to the device-width (no matter the device) and the initial scale to be set to 1.0 (no zoom).

<meta name="viewport" content="width=device-width, initial-scale=1.0">

Let's add this new meta tag element into our HTML, right after our after existing meta tag that sets the charset.

```
<> index.htm  X        # main.css         JS main.js

<> index.htm > ⊘ html > ⊘ head > ⊘ meta
 1      <!DOCTYPE html>
 2      <html lang="en">
 3          <head>
 4              <title>moji: manage your emojis</title>
 5              <meta charset="utf-8">
 6              <meta name="viewport" content="width=device-width, initial-scale=1.0">
 7              <link href="https://cdn.jsdelivr.net/npm/bootstrap@5.0.0-beta2/dist/css/bo
 8              <link href="css/main.css" rel="stylesheet">
 9              <script src="https://cdn.jsdelivr.net/npm/bootstrap@5.0.0-beta2/dist/js/bo
10              <script src="js/main.js"></script>
11          </head>
```

Now, go and refresh the page (CTRL-F5) in the browser and you will see that the iPhone view looks much better and will be usable.

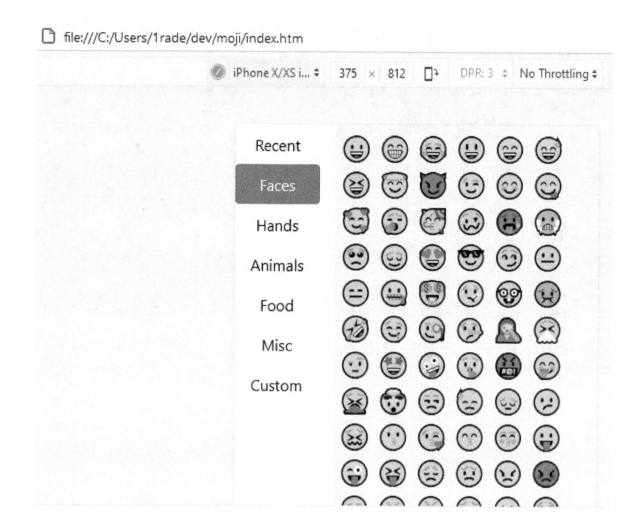

Isn't that fantastic? The buttons and the emojis all look great now and it will be possible to touch the correct item every time.

Viewable On Desktop Computers
Of course, this meta tag doesn't do anything bad to your desktop view either, so this is something we will want to include in all of our future web pages, because it makes web pages usable (responsive) across all devices.

You can read more about this meta tag on the MDN (Mozilla Dev Network):
https://developer.mozilla.org/en-US/docs/Web/HTML/Viewport_meta_tag

Get the Code : moji-14

I've checked the code into the Volume2\moji-14 directory so you can get it and examine the code and try it out in your own browser.

Development Is Iterative

Today's lesson has really displayed how that development is iterative. It is a cycle of adding a bit of code that gets basic things working and then adding one feature at a time. Sometimes when you see a huge application you wonder how the developers could create such and amazing thing. But just remember, they did it the same way: by using a process that just took each thing one step at a time. That's the best way forward.

To Build Anything: Just Start

That's also why if you want to build anything, you must simply start. Just decide on the best place to start and go from there. In the types of apps we are creating the start is often with just getting a static (unchanging) web page created -- using HTML. Next, we might start adding some styling to get the page looking like what we want it to look like -- CSS. Finally, we want to activate something or allow the user to interact with the page and that most likely requires JavaScript. See how they all work together?

We have solved quite a bit of what we want this moji app to do, but if you examine the Recent tab, you will see that we still have some static (unchanging) text there.

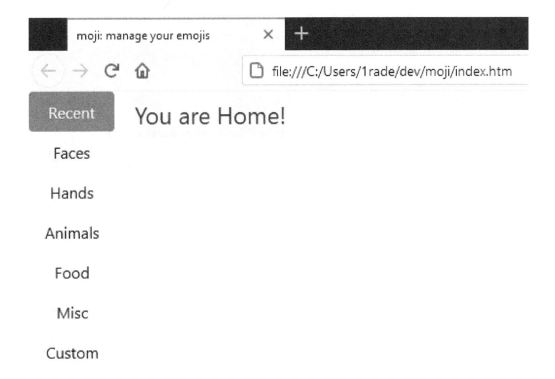

One More Thing: Unselecting Emojis

There is one more kind of annoying thing that we could fix today. It's the fact that if you select a bunch of emojis there is no fast way to unselect them all. Well, you can refresh the entire page and then nothing will be selected, but I'd rather provide the user with a button she can click to remove all the selected emojis because it will make our app feel more like a real app and not just a web page.

There's really only two steps we need to take.
1. Add a new button the user can click to unselect all emojis
2. Implement a few lines of code to unselect the emojis.

First, let's add another Bootstrap styled button at the bottom of all our other buttons.

This button will be inside the same outer div that holds all of our pill buttons, but it will not require an associated div for a tab display. This button is just going to active some code.

```
<button type="button" class="btn btn-warning"
onclick="unselectAll()">Unselect All</button>
```

If you compare this button to the others you will see that it has a btn-warning style added that the others do not have. This will simply cause the button to render in a yellow color. It's just a way to attempt to indicate to the user that this is not a emoji tab selection button like the other pills.

I've also added :
1. Unselect All as the text of the button
2. A function that will be called when the button is clicked.
   a. This is just an easy way to insure the code will be fired onclick. I could've done this by adding an event listener that loads when the page loads also. There are always many ways to get to the same solution in programming.

You can see the line of HTML that we added is the last button in the div.

```
<> index.htm ×    # main.css    JS main.js
<> index.htm > ⬡ html > ⬡ body > ⬡ div.d-flex.align-items-start > ⬡ div#v-pills-tab.nav.flex-column.nav-pills.me-3 > ⬡ button.btn.btn-warning
  1    CTYPE html>
  2    l lang="en">
  3    <head>
  4        <title>moji: manage your emojis</title>
  5        <meta charset="utf-8">
  6        <meta name="viewport" content="width=device-width, initial-scale=1.0">
  7        <link href="https://cdn.jsdelivr.net/npm/bootstrap@5.0.0-beta2/dist/css/bootstrap.min.css" rel="stylesh
  8        <link href="css/main.css" rel="stylesheet">
  9        <script src="https://cdn.jsdelivr.net/npm/bootstrap@5.0.0-beta2/dist/js/bootstrap.bundle.min.js" integr
 10        <script src="js/main.js"></script>
 11    </head>
 12    <body>
 13        <div class="d-flex align-items-start">
 14            <div class="nav flex-column nav-pills me-3" id="v-pills-tab" role="tablist" aria-orientation="verti
 15                <button class="nav-link" id="recent-pill" data-bs-toggle="pill" data-bs-target="#recent-tab" type
 16                <button class="nav-link active" id="faces-pill" data-bs-toggle="pill" data-bs-target="#faces-tab"
 17                <button class="nav-link" id="hands-pill" data-bs-toggle="pill" data-bs-target="#hands-tab" type="
 18                <button class="nav-link" id="animals-pill" data-bs-toggle="pill" data-bs-target="#animals-tab" ty
 19                <button class="nav-link" id="food-pill" data-bs-toggle="pill" data-bs-target="#food-tab" type="bu
 20                <button class="nav-link" id="misc-pill" data-bs-toggle="pill" data-bs-target="#misc-tab" type="bu
 21                <button class="nav-link" id="custom-pill" data-bs-toggle="pill" data-bs-target="#custom-tab" type
 22                <button type="button" class="btn btn-warning" onclick="unselectAll()">Unselect All</button>
 23            </div>
```

Now when we refresh the page you'll see the button. Of course it isn't wired up, because we haven't added the method (function) to our main.js yet, so it doesn't do anything.

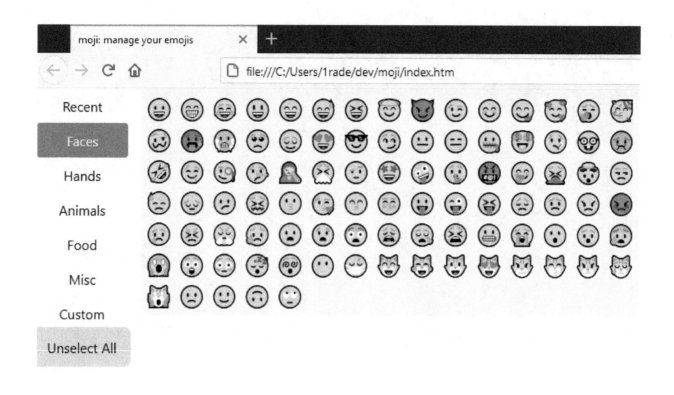

You can see that I tried clicking the button and the dev tools console give me an error because the function is not defined.

Let's add the simple code now.

I'll add the code as the last function in the main.js file.

It simply needs to do two things:
1. Remove all items from our allSelectedElements[] array.
2. Remove selection display from all emojis.

Here's how simple that code is:

```
function unselectAll(){
  allSelectedElements = [];
  window.getSelection().removeAllRanges();
}
```

To initialize any array to empty you can use the array initializer which is a set of opening and closing square brackets [ ] (included space so you can see each one).
This syntax (language rule) allows you to tell the JavaScript interpreter to set the allSelectedElements thing to an empty array. That solves the first thing we needed to do.

Browser's Window Object

Next, we
1. implement the browser's Window object
2. to call a function named getSelection()
3. getSelection() returns an object and we immediately call
4. removeAllRanges() on that returned object which removes the display of all selected items on screen.

If you look up Window.GetSelection() on the MDN (https://developer.mozilla.org/en-US/docs/Web/API/Window/getSelection) you'll see that it explains that the function returns a Selection object.

Window.getSelection()

The `Window.getSelection()` method returns a `Selection` object representing the range of text selected by the user or the current position of the caret.

Syntax

```
selection = window.getSelection();
```

Return value

A `Selection` object.

We could've written the code like:

```
let selObject = window.getSelection();
selObject.removeAllRanges();
```

Simpler Code Can Sometimes Be Confusing

But since we are not using the selObject any more, except to make the one call to removeAllRanges() we just do all of the code on that one line. The simpler written (one-line code) can be a bit more confusing though, if you've never seen it.

If you look up the Selection object on the MDN (https://developer.mozilla.org/en-US/docs/Web/API/Selection) you will get a list of all the Properties and Methods (functions) that the Selection object supports. These are all part of the Web API (Application Programming Interface) that the JavaScript developers have written the code for so you can easily do your work.

Under the Selection object Methods you'll see the removeAllRanges() method.

Selection.removeAllRanges()

⚗ Experimental

This is an experimental technology

Check the Browser compatibility table carefully before using this in production.

The `Selection.removeAllRanges()` method removes all ranges from the selection, leavi `anchorNode` and `focusNode` properties equal to `null` and leaving nothing selected.

Syntax

```
sel.removeAllRanges();
```

Parameters

None.

That explains everything about how this works. Now when the user clicks our button (if there are any emojis selected, they will all be unselected.

Also, if nothing is selected, the code will run but do nothing (but it also won't create an error).

Get the Code : Try It Out - moji-15

I've saved the code in the Volume2\moji-15 directory so you can get it and try it out.

We added a lot of functionality today, with some very small and simple code changes.
Keeping our code limited is a gift to ourselves in the future if we ever have to do maintenance.
It makes it so we have less code to look through so we can fix or enhance problems easier.

Tomorrow : localStorage

Tomorrow we will begin adding code which will remember which emojis the user has clicked on. This will introduce you to a very cool feature of the browser which allows you to store data in the user's browser storage area. The feature that can be implemented using JavaScript will store data on disk that can be read again but has some security limitations. The feature is called localStorage.

Day 51

We are now driving fast towards completing our emoji app. Let's consider our backlog again and mark off the ones which are complete. I've marked them with an [X] in the following list.

- [X] As a user, I want to be able to select any emoji so I can add it to a document I am writing.
- As a user, I want to be able to collect new emojis and add them into the program so I can use them later in documents I am writing.
- [X] As a user, I want to be able to view my emojis in categories so I can find the one I want more easily.
- As a user I want a list of my recently used emojis so I can find the one I want to use more easily.
- [X] As a user I want this program to run all the time on my desktop so I can easily copy an emoji and paste it into a document or post I am writing.

We have completed three of the five items.

Now we want to tackle the fourth item in the list -- view list of recently used emojis.

We already have the tab where we will display these, but how can we capture this list?

Capturing a List of Recently Used Emojis

I'm going to consider that a recently used emoji is simply one that has been clicked. This is not quite entirely correct, because we really need to know which ones are clicked and then copied, but this is close enough.

OnClick Already Handled

We know our onclick for each emoji is already handled so this will just be code that is added when an emoji is clicked. Since this code is going to do something different, it guides us into thinking that we are going to create at least one new function that will do the storing of this list for us.

Single Responsibility Principle

The Single Responsibility Principle is a guideline that is a part of the SOLID Principles (https://en.wikipedia.org/wiki/SOLID) which is an acronym for five principles that we try to follow when developing software. Keeping these principles in mind help us develop software that is better constructed and is more easily maintained and enhanced.

The Single Responsibility Principle tells us : a class (or function) should have a single thing that it does. This is a help in code organization. Keep in mind it is a principle. These are not laws. They are helpful things to keep in mind. They are guidance.

More Details of Recently Used

Our user stories that represent our backlog are not extremely detailed and that is fine. Sometimes we may be creating the code to create the solution for a backlog item and we just need to focus on getting the thing done as simply as possible. In this case, I know we want:
1. Each clicked emoji to appear on the recently used tab so the user can find it.
2. These need to persist even if the user re-loads the web page.
     a. If they didn't persist the recently used list would only last during the current session and that isn't very helpful.
     b. We are writing all client code -- code that runs in the browser so we have no way to store the list on a server. This leads us to browser storage techniques and I know that means localStorage.
3. The list should only add new items to the list so we don't get duplicates when the same emoji is clicked. This is a bit of a challenge.
4. The list should make sure that the newest used emojis are listed first. Reverse order of how they are pushed onto an array.

localStorage: Web Browser Storage Access

localStorage is a method that allows the web browser to save or read data from your disk (SSD Solid State* Device), HDD (Hard Disk Drive), etc)

NOTE: Solid State means no moving parts. SSDs are flash ram and contain no moving parts while HDDs are platters (like CDs) spinning inside the device.

Storage Access: Many Limitations

Allowing a browser to access a user's local disk is very dangerous because malware (malicious software) would be happy to store viruses etc there. This is why JavaScript developers and browser developers have included a lot of limitations on the localStorage abilities.
But, it is also why using the localStorage API is very secure and you don't have to worry about security as much since the web browser devs have handled most of the issues.

#1 localStorage Safety Item To Keep In Mind

The number one safety item to keep in mind can also feel like a huge limitation.
You cannot read the values from anywhere except where the values were originally written.

That means if you save items to localStorage from while running your page from the URL:
c:\users\<username>\dev\moji\ then you can only access the data when the page is loaded from that same URL.

This is kind of odd to talk about because we aren't loading from a true web server (that'll happen in Volume3) but this also means that only the web site (URL) that wrote values to your localStorage can read those values.

True For All Web Sites
This means that microsoft.com cannot read the values that google.com saved in localStorage and vice versa. This is fantastically important because if you have your web site write values to localStorage, you don't want another web site (possibly malicious) to be able to read those values.

#2 localStorage Limitation: Only Current Web Browser

If your user goes to your website on ComputerA and your website stores info in localStorage then only that exact browser on ComputerA can retrieve those values.

For example suppose you have FireFox and Chrome on ComputerA.
You open FireFox on ComputerA and navigate to raddev.us (my website) and it stores data in your localStorage.
Now, you open Chrome on ComputerA and navigate to raddev.us and you try to read the values that were stored before (when you ran FireFox). That will fail. That's because the localStorage is URL and browser specific. They do not share.

What Does This Mean To Us?
This means that your recently used list will be tied to
1. a device (computer, phone, etc)
2. And tied to the browser you used on that device.

That means if the user uses FireFox on ComputerA and then forgets and uses Chrome then her recently used list will be completely different.

The Next Level: Servers & User Login

This is a limitation of localStorage that can only be solved by using a Web Server and having a user create a login -- personal account that stores this data.

Teaches Limitations and Better Understanding of Challenges

But, keep in mind, we are creating an app that is just a quick easy app that we use to quickly copy / paste emojis. It's not a big deal. I've also done it this way so you can see the limitations of browser technology so that you understand why we need to implement web server technology later on.

We're also using localStorage, because it is so easy to use. It's far more difficult to persist data to a web server and a database (much more technology involved and more things we need to know how to do).

If these limitations don't make sense right now, as we go along you will see what they mean.

localStorage: Very Easy To Use

Let's try localStorage right now.

1. Load the current moji app in your web browser
2. Open your Dev Console (F12)
3. Run the following localStorage command to store a string
   a. `localStorage.setItem("first", "first is best");`

That will look something like the following:

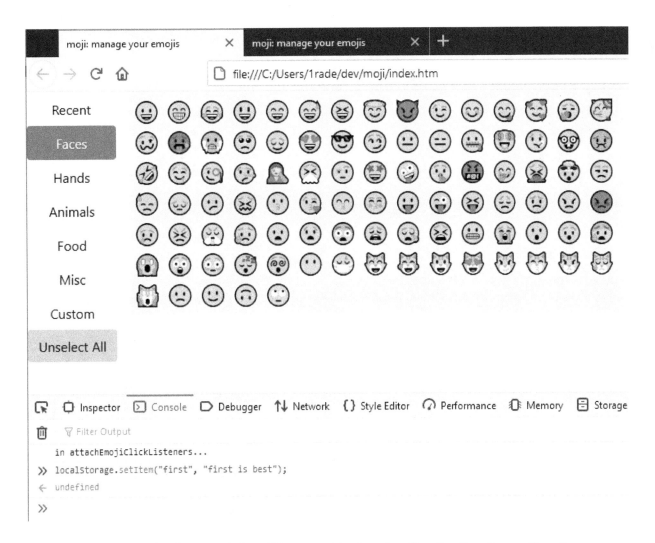

We are referencing the browser's localStorage object and calling the function setItem().

setItem takes two parameters:

1. String name of item you are storing -- you will use this name to retrieve the value later
2. String value that you want to store.

Name / Value Pairs

It's really just name value pairs again.

Let's retrieve the value we stored.

```
localStorage.getItem("first");
```

```
⊡  Inspector  ▣ Console  ⬭ Debugger  ↑↓ Network  {}

🗑  ▽ Filter Output
```

```
   in attachEmojiClickListeners...
≫  localStorage.setItem("first", "first is best");
←  undefined
≫  localStorage.getItem("first");
←  "first is best"
≫  |
```

You can see that the console prints the value of the item: "first is best" The double-quotes indicate that it is a string value. We could've stored the value of the item in a variable.

```
≫  let first = localStorage.getItem("first");
←  undefined
≫  first
←  "first is best"
≫
```

Everything Stored in localStorage Becomes A String

No matter what you store in localStorage, it gets turned into a string when you store it.

For example if we store a boolean value of true (which isn't a string) into localStorage, then localStorage will automatically convert it to a string.

I've done this in the console with a number of commands to show you this.

```
>> let myBool = true;
<- undefined
>> localStorage.setItem("firstBool", myBool);
<- undefined
>> typeof myBool
<- "boolean"
>> let boolFromStorage = localStorage.getItem("firstBool");
<- undefined
>> typeof boolFromStorage
<- "string"
>> boolFromStorage
<- "true"
>>
```

First I created a boolean type and set it to the value of true (not the string true -- there are no double-quotes around the value).
Next I store the value in localStorage and name it firstBool.
I then show you that the browser understands that the typeof myBool is a boolean (using the typeof operator).

After that I retrieve the value of the firstBool from localStorage and save it to a new variable named boolFromStorage.
Finally, we check the type that comes back from storage is: typeof boolFromStorage.
The browser reports that it is a string.
Finally, notice that boolFromStorage does contain the value of "true" but it is the string value (double-quoted) and not the true value. Of course these are different values.

The point of all of this is that everything that is stored in localStorage and may need to be converted back to the type you want to use it as -- if it is not a string type of thing.

In our case with emojis, they are characters which make up strings so everything should work fine.

addEmojiToRecentList() : New Function

Let's add a new function to main.js which we will call whenever an emoji is clicked and added to the selected list.

We'll call this function addEmojiToRecentList() and we'll pass the function the emoji we want to add to the list.

Here's what the function will look like before we fill it out with code.

```
addEmojiToRecentList(emoji){
}
```

Let's also add a call to this function in our emoji click handler.

We'll use the innerHTML property to pass just the emoji character to our new function.

Here's what it will look like:

```
addEmojiToRecentList(el.innerHTML);
```

You can see it here on line 27:

```
<> index.htm          # main.css          JS main.js          ●

js > JS main.js > ⊗ handleEmojiClick
    17              }) // end of addEventListener function
    18          } // end of for/of
    19      } // end of function
    20
    21      function handleEmojiClick(el) {
    22          if (isSelected(el)){
    23              removeElement(el);
    24          }
    25          else{
    26              allSelectedElements.push(el);
    27              addEmojiToRecentList(el.innerHTML);
    28          }
    29          displaySelectedElements();
    30      }
```

We'll need a new array to hold our list of newly selected emojis. I'll add it to the top of main.js to make it globally accessible to all the functions in main.js.

```
let recentlyUsedEmojis = [];
```

Now, we have the structure of what we need and we just need to write the code to add new emojis to our list and ignore emojis that are already in our list. Let's start writing our addEmojiToRecentList() function.

First I'll fill out the function with some comments that will represent the work we want to do so we can plan what we want.

function addEmojiToRecentList(emoji){
  // 1. determine if the emoji is a new one - if it isn't then

```
  // return out of this method because there is nothing more
  // to do since the emoji has already been added to recent list
  if (isEmojiNew(emoji,recentlyUsedEmojis) == false){
    return;
  }
// 2. do the work to display the recent emojis
// this will require some work to add new spans to our DOM.
// Yes, you can add new HTML elements to the DOM dynamically with JS
  displayRecentEmojis(emoji);

  // if the emoji isn't already in the list, then add it and save
  // it to localStorage.
  // 3. Push the emoji on the array we are using to track this list
  recentlyUsedEmojis.push(emoji);
// 4. We need to only allow this list to get so large because we only want the last
// X number of recent emojis used so we use a number like 50.
  if (recentlyUsedEmojis.length > RECENTLY_USED_MAX){
    recentlyUsedEmojis.shift();
  }
  // 5. Finally, we use a method (JSON.stringify) to turn our array into a string
// that we can store in localStorage.  You must stringify the array or you won't
// be able to turn it back into an array later.
  localStorage.setItem("recentEmojis", JSON.stringify(recentlyUsedEmojis));
}
```

```
33    function addEmojiToRecentList(emoji){
34       // 1. determine if the emoji is a new one - if it isn't then
35       // return out of this method because there is nothing more
36       // to do since the emoji has already been added to recent list
37       if (isEmojiNew(emoji,recentlyUsedEmojis) == false){
38          return;
39       }
40       // 2. do the work to display the recent emojis
41       // this will require some work to add new spans to our DOM.
42       // Yes, you can add new HTML elements to the DOM dynamically with JS
43       displayRecentEmojis(emoji);
44
45       // if the emoji isn't already in the list, then add it and save
46       // it to localStorage.
47       // 3. Push the emoji on the array we are using to track this list
48       recentlyUsedEmojis.push(emoji);
49       // 4. We need to only allow this list to get so large because we only want the last
50       // X number of recent emojis used so we use a number like 50.
51       if (recentlyUsedEmojis.length > RECENTLY_USED_MAX){
52          recentlyUsedEmojis.shift();
53       }
54       // 5. Finally, we use a method (JSON.stringify) to turn our array into a string
55       // that we can store in localStorage.  You must stringify the array or you won't
56       // be able to turn it back into an array later.
57       localStorage.setItem("recentEmojis", JSON.stringify(recentlyUsedEmojis));
58    }
```

Now, we need to add our supporting functions:
1. isEmojiNew()
2. displayRecentEmojis()

We simply need to iterate through every emoji in the recentlyUsedEmojis array and determine if the emoji is in the array or not.

```
function isEmojiNew(emoji){
  for (let i = 0; i < recentlyUsedEmojis.length;i++){
   if (recentlyUsedEmojis[i] === emoji){
     // if the emoji is already in the list
     // then just return -- this is a quick exit
     // from the function when the emoji is found
     // early in the list
     console.log("returning...")
     return false;
   }
  }
  // The code will only get to here
  // if the emoji wasn't found in the list.
  // We return true that it is a new emoji.
  return true;
```

```
   }

60   function isEmojiNew(emoji){
61      for (let i = 0; i < recentlyUsedEmojis.length;i++){
62         if (recentlyUsedEmojis[i] === emoji){
63            // if the emoji is already in the list
64            // then just return -- this is a quick exit
65            // from the function when the emoji is found
66            // early in the list
67            console.log("returning...")
68            return false;
69         }
70      }
71      // The code will only get to here
72      // if the emoji wasn't found in the list.
73      // We return true that it is a new emoji.
74      return true;
75   }
```

This is kind of a brute-force way of determining whether or not the emoji is in the list, but it works and since there will only ever be a max of 50 items it is extremely fast.

This was a lot of code, so let's pick up again tomorrow with the writing the displayRecentEmojis() function.

Get the Code: But Not Complete Yet

You can get the code in the volume2\moji-16a directory, but keep in mind that it is not entirely working yet. We will do the work to complete this code tomorrow.

Day 52

Displaying Dynamic Content

The emojis we've added so far have all been added as static (unchanging) items in our HTML. We've added those one time to our HTML as spans and they always load in the same order and on the same tab. The content for our Recent tab will continually change as the user selects different emojis.

This means we need a way to generate content for our Recent tab that can be updated at any time (each time the user selects a new emoji).

JavaScript Can Create DOM Elements

Using JavaScript it is possible to create DOM elements dynamically.
This means that we can add content to our pages right in front of the user's eyes.

Let me show you what I mean. I think this functionality will amaze you. It amazed me when I first saw it. It kind of opens up everything because you can do anything on the page when you can add elements.

Follow these steps and we'll use the Browser's Dev Console to insert some new content on our page which will appear in front of your eyes.

Here's the code to copy and paste into your browser's dev console:

```
1. const newSpan = document.createElement("span");
2. newSpan.innerHTML = "This is our test text";
3. document.querySelector("#recent-tab").prepend(newSpan);
4. newSpan.addEventListener("click", ()=>{alert("it's on!")});
```

There's nothing here that you don't already understand. The is a new call to the document object function named createElement() but even that is fairly straight forward.

Here's what the code does:
1) Calls createElement("span") with a string parameter of the element type we want to create -- stores it in a const named newSpan so we can use it again.
   a) Note: At this point the element is created but not added to the DOM so the user can't see it.
2) We use innerHTML to set the content that will be displayed in the span ("This is our test text").

155

3) We call the familiar document.querySelector and reference our "#recent-tab" (the content area that is shown when the Recent button is clicked.
   a) Calling querySelector() selects the element object and then when it is returned we call the prepend() method and pass our newly created span to it.
   b) At this point the span is displayed (see next image below) and you'll see the text in your browser (after you click the Recent button).
4) Finally, we even add an eventListener to the span (just to show you what is possible) so that if you click the new span, it will pop up a message with "it's on!".

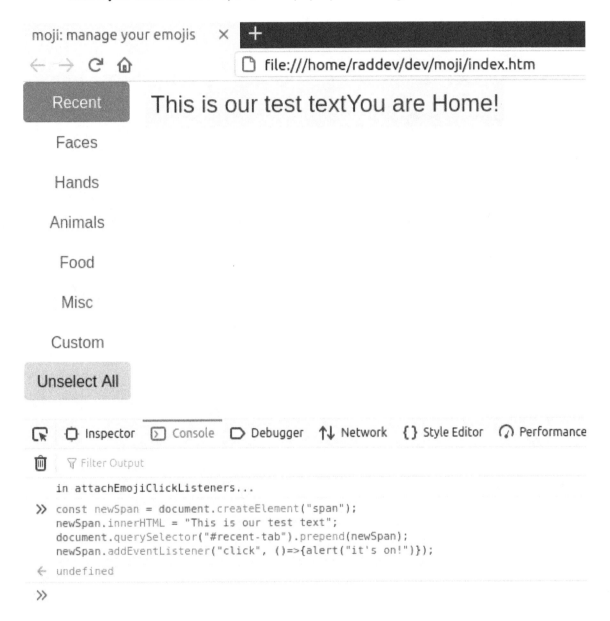

Of course, it isn't very pretty, because we prepended a span to the content that is already there, but it's really cool how it works. Go ahead and click somewhere in the new span.

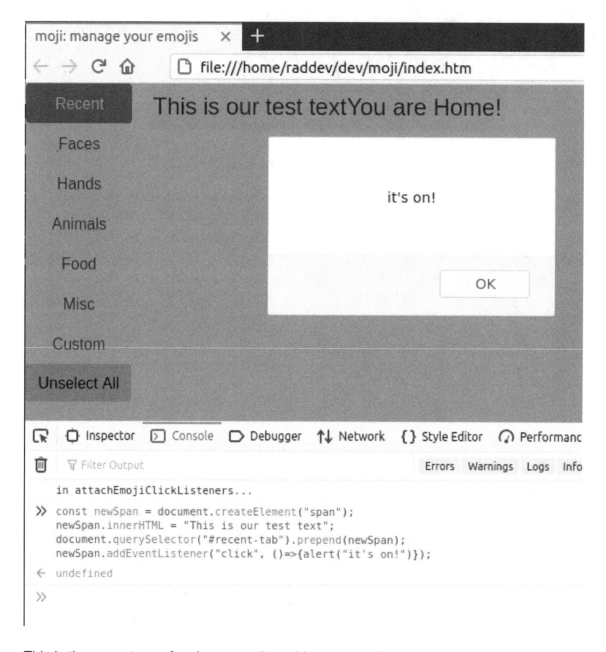

This is the same type of code we need to add to our emoji app except we want to:

1. Add it when the user selects a new emoji
2. Set the innerHTML to the emoji which was clicked -- so the user sees the list of emojis which have been used.
3. Add the handleEmojiClick() on each emoji which is added to the recent list. That way when the recent emoji is selected it will work exactly as other emojis do.

displaySelectedElements(): Add Content to the DOM

We are going to call our function displaySelectedElements(). We previously already added a call to that method in our handleEmojiClick() function but we haven't added code to it yet.

However, now that you've seen the sample you will see that the code is hardly different and quite easy to understand.

```
function displayRecentEmojis(emoji){
  const newSpan = document.createElement("span");
  newSpan.innerHTML = emoji;
  // the call to prepend() allows me to use normal forward iteration
  // thru the array but shows the most recently added emoji
  // (highest index) first.
  document.querySelector("#recent-tab").prepend(newSpan);
  newSpan.addEventListener("click", handleEmojiClick);
}
```

```
23   function handleEmojiClick(el) {
24       if (isSelected(el)){
25           removeElement(el);
26       }
27       else{
28           allSelectedElements.push(el);
29           addEmojiToRecentList(el.innerHTML);
30       }
31       displaySelectedElements(el.innerHTML);
32   }
33
34   function displayRecentEmojis(emoji){
35       const newSpan = document.createElement("span");
36       newSpan.innerHTML = emoji;
37       // the call to prepend() allows me to use normal forward iteration
38       // thru the array but shows the most recently added emoji
39       // (highest index) first.
40       document.querySelector("#recent-tab").prepend(newSpan);
41       newSpan.addEventListener("click", handleEmojiClick);
42   }
```

One More Thing

Don't forget to remove the static text we had on the recent-tab in the HTML (You are Home!) because we don't need that placeholder text any more.

```
21   utton class="nav-link" id="custom-pill" data-bs-toggle="pill" data-bs-target="#custom-tab" type="button" role="
22   utton type="button" class="btn btn-warning" onclick="unselectAll()">Unselect All</button>
23   v>
24     class="tab-content" id="v-pills-tabContent">
25   <div class="tab-pane fade emoji" id="recent-tab" role="tabpanel" aria-labelledby="recent-tab">You are Home!</di
26   <div class="tab-pane fade emoji show active" id="faces-tab" role="tabpanel" aria-labelledby="faces-tab">
27       <span>&#128512;</span>
28       <span>&#128513;</span>
```

Try It Out: Volume2\moji-16b

You can get the updated code in the Volume2\moji-16b folder.

If you've been following along and adding the code, just refresh (CTRL-F5) your page in the browser and then click some emojis. After you click some emojis, click the Recent button and you'll see the emojis that you've just clicked with the most recent one first.

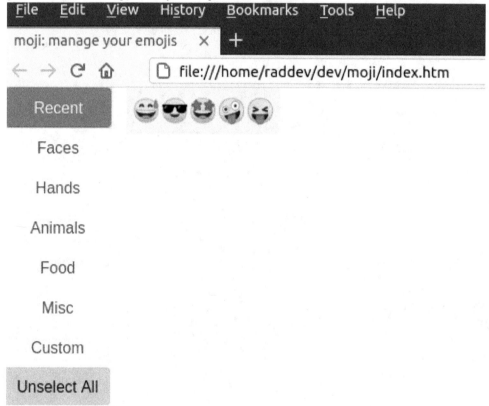

One More Thing: Reloading the Recent List
There's just one more thing we need to fix for this functionality to be complete. We've saved the emoji list to localStorage, but we haven't added a function that adds them back to the Recent tab when we reload (refresh) the page. You will see that if you refresh the page, then your Recent list will be gone. Even though your emojis are saved to localStorage.

You can see the list of emojis that were saved by opening your Dev Console and typing : localStorage and pressing enter.

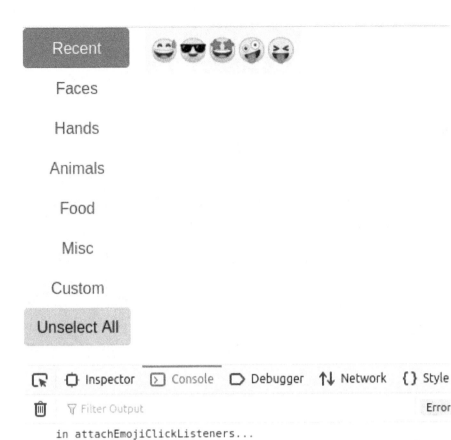

Let's fix the reload problem now.
We just need to add another function that runs when the page is loaded. It needs to load the emojis from localStorage so we will call it: loadRecentsFromLocalStorage().

First we add our new function:

```
function loadRecentsFromLocalStorage(){
  recentlyUsedEmojis = JSON.parse(localStorage.getItem("recentEmojis"));
  if (recentlyUsedEmojis === null){
      // if null set to an empty array,
    // so array can later be pushed to
    recentlyUsedEmojis = [];
    return;
  }
  recentlyUsedEmojis.forEach(emoji => {
      displayRecentEmojis(emoji);
  });
}
```

```
44   function loadRecentsFromLocalStorage(){
45       // First we load the item we stored in localStorage but we need to call parse()
46       // on it so it will be turned back into an array.  If we don't, it'll be a string.
47       recentlyUsedEmojis = JSON.parse(localStorage.getItem("recentEmojis"));
48       // Next, we check to see if the array is null because if there are no
49       // items stored in localStorage named "recentEmojis" then the JSON.parse() will
50       // return a null value.  if it is null there is nothing left to do, so
51       // we return from the function.
52       if (recentlyUsedEmojis === null){
53           // if null set to an empty array,
54           // so array can later be pushed to
55           recentlyUsedEmojis = [];
56           return;
57       }
58       // if there are some emojis then they've been loaded into our array
59       // Now we iterate through them and call the displayRecentEmojis()
60       // which will display them in the Recent tab.
61       recentlyUsedEmojis.forEach(emoji => {
62           displayRecentEmojis(emoji);
63       });
64   }
```

JSON.parse() Function

Notice that when we retrieve the recentEmojis item from localStorage that we do not just store the returned value in our recentlyUsedEmojis variable (which needs to be an array). Instead, we call a function (JSON.parse()) on the string that is returned from localStorage.getItem(). JSON.parse() is a JavaScript API method provided by the JavaScript developers.

JSON is an acronym which stands for JavaScript Object Notation. The JSON.parse() method takes a valid JSON string and parses it into an object. In our case it turns it into an array of one character strings which represent each emoji.

Expecting Array

If we hadn't called JSON.parse() on the item then we would've instead received a string of emoji characters and other operations where we are expecting an array would've failed. This is inherently related to the way we designed the other methods.
Back in our addEmojiToRecentList() function we had the following line of code which used JSON.stringify() to turn our array into a JSON string before storing it in localStorage:

```
localStorage.setItem("recentEmojis", JSON.stringify(recentlyUsedEmojis));
```

These two functions (JSON.stringify() & JSON.parse()) work together: the first to turn our Array into a valid string of JSON and the second to turn our Object into a valid JSON string.

A New Challenge Arises

This new method needs to be called when the main.js file loads. Well, that isn't quite exactly right. It really needs to be called after the HTML <body> element is completely loaded. Why?

The reason our new method loadRecentsFromLocalStorage() cannot run until onload has completed is because it calls displayRecentEmojis() and that method is dependent upon the DOM being loaded and the recent-tab element being available. If it isn't and the displayRecentEmojis() method fires then it will fail when the method calls querySelector() on the recent tab.

Cannot Add Function To Top of main.js

If we simply add the method to the top of main.js and attempt to run we will see an error like the following (because the DOM isn't completely done loading before the method is called):

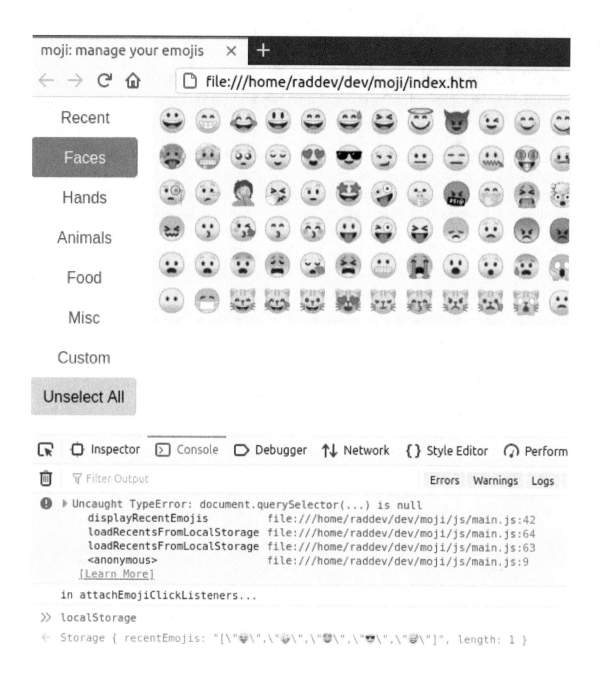

To solve this the easiest (but not necessarily the best) way we can just add the call to the method in the HTML on the body onload event.

```
 9            <script src="https://cdn.jsdelivr.net/npm/bootstrap@5.0
10            <script src="js/main.js"></script>
11        </head>
12  |     <body onload="loadRecentsFromLocalStorage()">
13            <div class="d-flex align-items-start">
14                <div class="nav flex-column nav-pills me-3" id="v-p
15                    <button class="nav-link" id="recent-pill" data-bs
16                    <button class="nav-link active" id="faces-pill" d
17                    <button class="nav-link" id="hands-pill" data-bs-
```

Now the method will not be called until the entire body of the document is loaded and it will work properly.

Now my recents load after I refresh the page.

Get the Code: Volume2\moji-16c

Try the code out. If you've been following along just refresh your browser and select some emojis. They should show up in your recent list. Refresh the page again and check the Recent tab and they should still show up since they are reloaded from localStorage.

We just have one more things to complete for our app to fulfill all of our User Stories from our original Backlog.

- [ ] As a user, I want to be able to collect new emojis and add them into the program so I can use them later in documents I am writing.

But, I'm going to add one more fun thing to the backlog. I want the user to be able to toggle the size of the Emojis from the x-large size to xx-large size so we're going to add a button which will allow that too. We'll store the value that represents the state (size of emojis) in localStorage so that once the user sets the value it will stay until she toggles it to the other size.

Day 53

One More localStorage List

The code to add new (custom) emojis to our app is very similar to the code we used for the Recent list. That's because we want to store the custom emojis in localStorage so they are always available to the user -- so that part is the same as the Recent list.

The only difference really is that we need to provide the user with a place to paste their custom emoji in so we can store it in localStorage and make it available to the user when she runs our app.

We basically need something like the following for the UI (User Interface):

The user will be able to paste her emoji into the text box and click the Save button. Clicking the Save button will do two things:
1. Make sure that the emoji hasn't already been saved in the custom emoji list.
2. If it hasn't already been saved, it will be saved to localStorage.

First, we need to add our new HTML (text box and button) to Custom tab.
I searched on the Bootstrap site for a sample like the one above and found the code and grabbed it.

The reason I knew about this is simply because I've browsed around on the site and tried these kinds of things before. In Bootstrap parlance this is called an input group.

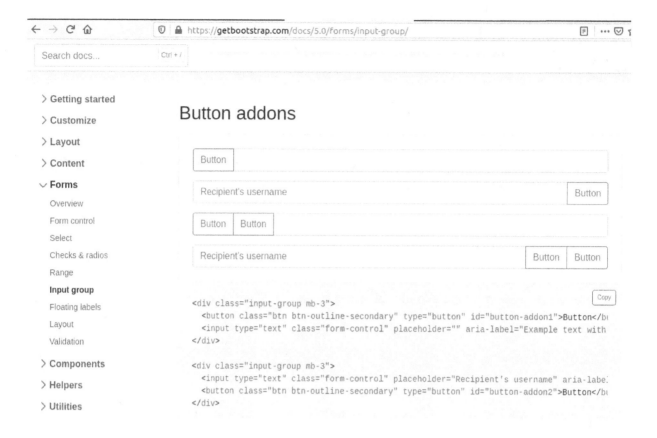

Placeholder Style

The special text that appears in the text box to instruct the user what the box is used for is the placeholder text. It's just a simple attribute of the <input type="text"> that does this for you. It's very nice because it means you don't have to take up valuable screen space for a label.

Here's the HTML with bootstrap styling that we are adding to our Custom tab on index.htm.

```
<div class="input-group mb-3">
    <input id="customEmojiText"type="text" class="form-control" placeholder="Add emojis here"
aria-label="Add emojis here" aria-describedby="saveCustomEmoji">
    <button id="saveCustomEmoji" class="btn btn-outline-primary" type="button" >Save</button>
</div>
```

```
293        <div class="tab-pane fade emoji" id="custom-tab" role="tabpanel" aria-labelledby="custom-tab">
294            <div class="input-group mb-3">
295                <input id="customEmojiText"type="text" class="form-control" placeholder="Add emojis here"
296                <button id="saveCustomEmoji" class="btn btn-outline-primary" type="button" >Save</button>
297            </div>
298        </div>
```

Even though it looks like a lot of confusing code (because of all the crazy Bootstrap attributes) if you stay focused on the main elements you will see that you already know everything you need to know.

We've really just added:
1. 1 <div>
2. 1 <input type="text">
3. 1 <button>

You know all about those. The rest of the stuff is just the Bootstrap styling that will make it so the button is at the end of the text box. This is also nice because it immediately communicates to the user what she is saving.

Everything else will still work the same but if you go to the Custom tab now you will see something like the following.

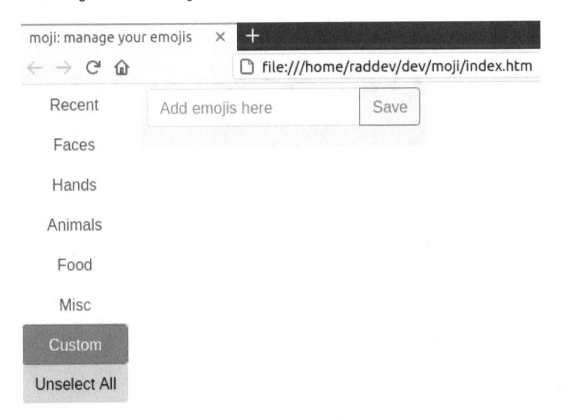

To get this button to do something let's add an eventListener for the click of the button at the top of main.js.

Initialize Application
However, since we are beginning to have quite a few things that need to load and run after the entire page loads, let's switch up and :
1. Create an initApp() function
2. Add all of the things that will run when the page loads to the initApp() function so they can all be found in one place.
3. Update the <body onload="loadRecentsFromLocalStorage()"> to call initApp() instead.

Here's the new initApp() function with all of the items added to it.

```
function initApp(){
  // this selector makes it so currently selected emojis are not unselected.
  document.querySelector("html").addEventListener("click",
      ()=>displaySelectedElements());
document.querySelector("#saveCustomEmoji").addEventListener("click",
    saveCustoEmojiHandler);

  loadRecentsFromLocalStorage();
}
```

Here's the top of main.js with the global variables we need and the initApp() function that is now loaded when <body> onload fires.

```
JS main.js  X    <> index.htm

js > JS main.js > ⊕ attachEmojiClickListeners > [∅] allNodes
  1    addEventListener("load",attachEmojiClickListeners);
  2    const RECENTLY_USED_MAX = 50;
  3    let allSelectedElements = [];
  4    let recentlyUsedEmojis = [];
  5
  6
  7    function initApp(){
  8      // this selector makes it so currently selected emojis are not unselected.
  9      document.querySelector("html").addEventListener("click", ()=>displaySelectedElements());
 10      document.querySelector("#saveCustomEmoji").addEventListener("click",saveCustomEmojiHandler);
 11
 12      loadRecentsFromLocalStorage();
 13    }
 14
```

This helps us control everything we need to initialize in our app and cleans up the code so in the future we can easily know what is loading and running when the app loads.

Back To saveCustomEmojiHandler

Of course, we also need to add a (temporarily empty) new function named saveCustomEmojiHandler()) to our main.js.

I'm adding it to the bottom of the main.js file so I can find it and edit it easily.

```
function saveCustomEmojiHandler(){
}
```

Get User Input

The first thing I'd like to do is get the text (one or more emoji characters) that the user has input into the text box.

Get Text From Input Text Box

We know how to do this (from Volume 1) using the querySelector() and the .value property of the input element.

```
document.querySelector("#customEmojiText").value
```

However, if we get the text like that, it will be a simple string and I'd like to get the data as an Array.
Fortunately there is a JS built-in function of the Array object that will do this for us.
We simply wrap the previous code in the Array.from() function call and it will return the string as an array of characters which will be easy to iterate through.

We'll store it in a local variable named allUserAddedEmojis.

```
let allUserAddedEmojis =
Array.from(document.querySelector("#customEmojiText").value);
```

Informing the User

Immediately after getting the text from the user I want to empty out the text box so that it will inform the user that the app has taken the input and is working on it.

```
document.querySelector("#customEmojiText").value = "";
```

Doing this also helps so the user doesn't attempt to submit the same emojis a second time.

Next, we simply need to iterate through the characters in the Array and do some work on them.

Using Pseudo-Code To Think Things Through

Here's some pseudo-code (code-like language) that will help us work through the ideas we need to support. Some will be actual code and other will be something close just so we can think through

```
let atLeastOneDuplicate = false;  // set up a flag to determine if there is a
duplicate emoji
```

```
for (let i = 0; i < allUserAddedEmojis.length;i++){
    // get the current emoji (emoji at index i)
    let emoji = allUserAddedEmojis[i];
    if (isEmojiNew(emoji,customEmojis)){
      // if it's new, push it onto the list and write to to localstorage
      customEmojis.push(emoji);
      localStorage.setItem("customEmojis", JSON.stringify(customEmojis));
      displayCustomEmojis(emoji);
    }
    else{
      atLeastOneFailure = true;
    }
}
```

Because I wrote this out I see that there is a function (isEmojiNew) that is exactly like what we did when we checked if an emoji was a duplicate in the Recent list.
Instead of writing another function that does the same thing but works with another array we need to change our earlier function so it works with any array passed to it.
This is what is called refactoring.

Refactoring Means Altering Code To Make it Better

Let's change the original function isEmojiNew() so it will take two things:
1. A single emoji character
2. a generically named array (which will be tested to see if it includes the emoji character)

Just so we can keep in mind what we had, here is the original isEmojiNew() function:

```
99    function isEmojiNew(emoji){
100      for (let i = 0; i < recentlyUsedEmojis.length;i++){
101        if (recentlyUsedEmojis[i] === emoji){
102          // if the emoji is already in the list
103          // then just return -- this is a quick exit
104          // from the function when the emoji is found
105          // early in the list
106          console.log("returning...")
107          return false;
108        }
109      }
110      // The code will only get to here
111      // if the emoji wasn't found in the list.
112      // We return true that it is a new emoji.
113      return true;
114    }
```

Notice that on lines 100 and 101 it uses the recentlyUsedEmojis array to do the comparison.

We want the new function to use any array which is passed into the function to do the comparison.

Here's how easy it is to change the function:

```
99    function isEmojiNew(emoji, targetArray){
100       for (let i = 0; i < targetArray.length;i++){
101          if (targetArray[i] === emoji){
102             // if the emoji is already in the list
103             // then just return -- this is a quick exit
104             // from the function when the emoji is found
105             // early in the list
106             console.log("returning...")
107             return false;
108          }
109       }
110       // The code will only get to here
111       // if the emoji wasn't found in the list.
112       // We return true that it is a new emoji.
113       return true;
114    }
```

You can see we now (on line 99) pass in the array as targetArray and then on lines 100 and 101 we use that new name to refer to thet array.

Huge Win! Generic Code

We've just made this code more generic so it can be used in more cases and we've limited our code so that we don't have two different functions that do nearly the same thing. This is a huge win.

Now, we just need to make sure we alter our original call (from addEmojiToRecentList()) to this method to include the Array parameter. Then the isEmojiNew() function will work for both lists.

Add the new customEmojis[] array to the top of main.js so we have a global array we can access from anywhere in our main.js

let customEmojis = [];

Here's what our saveCustomEmojiHandler looks like so far.

```
154    function saveCustomEmojiHandler(){
155      let allUserAddedEmojis = Array.from(document.querySelector("#customEmojiText").value);
156      document.querySelector("#customEmojiText").value = "";
157      let atLeastOneFailure = false;
158      for (let i = 0; i < allUserAddedEmojis.length;i++){
159        let emoji = allUserAddedEmojis[i];
160        if (isEmojiNew(emoji, customEmojis)){
161          // if it's new, push it onto the list and write to to localstorage
162          customEmojis.push(emoji);
163          localStorage.setItem("customEmojis", JSON.stringify(customEmojis));
164          displayCustomEmojis(emoji);
165        }
166        else{
167          atLeastOneFailure = true;
168        }
169      }
170    }
```

Need To Add displayCustomEmojis()

Next, we just need to add the displayCustomEmojis() function to display our newly added emojis and we'll be able to test.

displayCustomEmojis() Very Similar to displayRecentEmojis()

We are going to use the displayRecentEmojis() as template for this new method.

```
function displayCustomEmojis(emoji){
  const newSpan = document.createElement("span");
  newSpan.innerHTML = emoji;
  // set id to custom so that later we can use it to determine
  // if it is an item which can be added to the recently used list.
  newSpan.id = "custom";
  // the call to prepend() allows me to use normal forward iteration
  // thru the array but shows the most recently added emoji
  // (highest index) first.
  document.querySelector("#custom-tab").appendChild(newSpan);
  newSpan.addEventListener("click", handleEmojiClick);
}
```

At this point we have everything we need to test it out. But not quite everything. Let's try it out anyways, because we've added a lot of code.

Test It Out

You can get the code in the Volume2\moji-17 directory.

Here are the steps I took to test this code.

1. Go to https://emojipedia.org/sparkles/ and click the copy button to copy the sparkles emoji. I'm doing the sparkles and the unicorn : ☐ ☐
2. Come back to our app with the changes and click Custom button so you can get to the proper functionality.
3. Paste one or more emojis into the input text box. (see first image below)
4. Click the [Save] button and you'll see something like what is shown in the second image below.

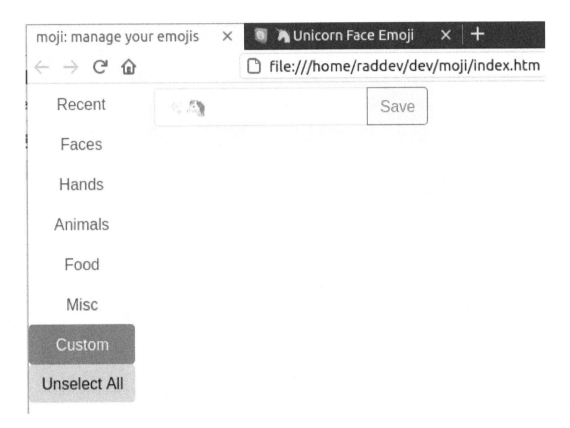

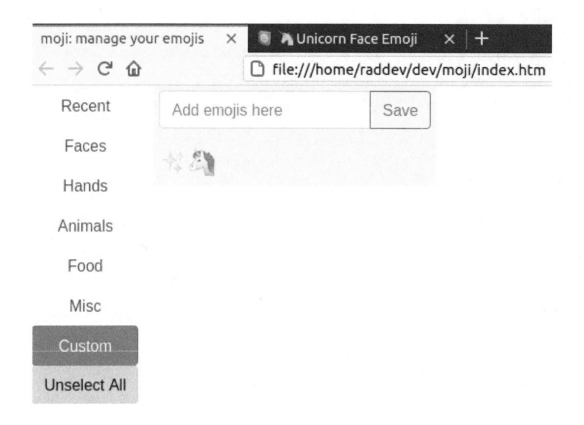

After clicking [Save] the displayCustomEmojis is called and the emojis are displayed as you expect.

Refresh: The Custom Emojis Disappear

However, if you refresh the page and click the Custom button again, you will see that the newly added items seem to have disappeared.

They really were saved to localStorage. You can see them in localStorage if you open the Dev Console in your web browser (F12) and type localStorage you'll see the item.

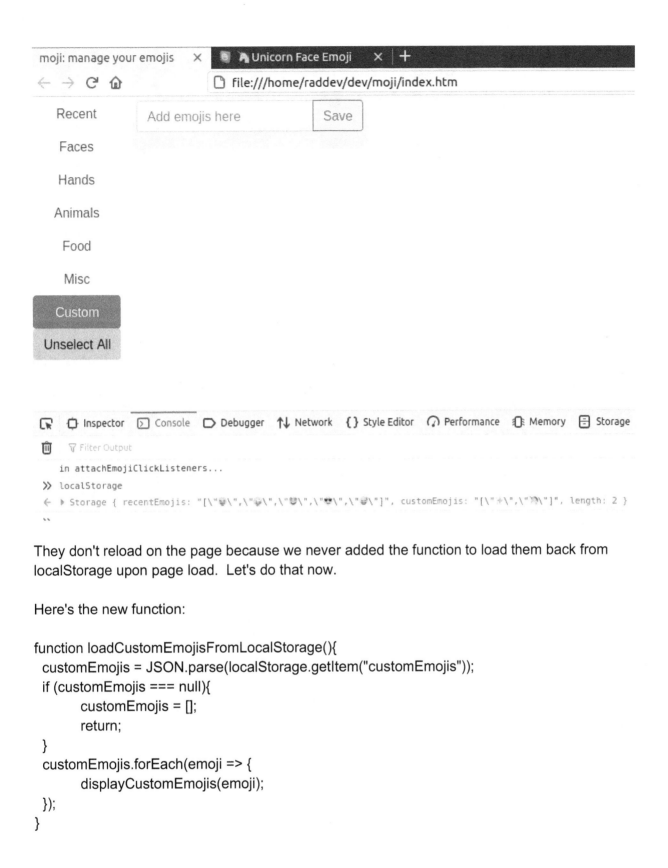

They don't reload on the page because we never added the function to load them back from localStorage upon page load. Let's do that now.

Here's the new function:

```
function loadCustomEmojisFromLocalStorage(){
  customEmojis = JSON.parse(localStorage.getItem("customEmojis"));
  if (customEmojis === null){
      customEmojis = [];
      return;
  }
  customEmojis.forEach(emoji => {
      displayCustomEmojis(emoji);
  });
}
```

```
186   function loadCustomEmojisFromLocalStorage(){
187     customEmojis = JSON.parse(localStorage.getItem("customEmojis"));
188     if (customEmojis === null){
189       customEmojis = [];
190       return;
191     }
192     customEmojis.forEach(emoji => {
193       displayCustomEmojis(emoji);
194     });
195   }
```

Once you add that code and the call to the code in our initApp() then all you have to do is refresh and you'll see the custom emojis displayed on the Custom tab.

```
8    function initApp(){
9      // this selector makes it so currently selected emojis are not unselected.
10     document.querySelector("html").addEventListener("click", ()=>displaySelectedElements());
11     document.querySelector("#saveCustomEmoji").addEventListener("click",saveCustomEmojiHandler);
12
13     loadRecentsFromLocalStorage();
14     loadCustomEmojisFromLocalStorage();
15   }
```

Get the Code: moji-18

Get the code in the Volume2/moji-18 directory and try it out.

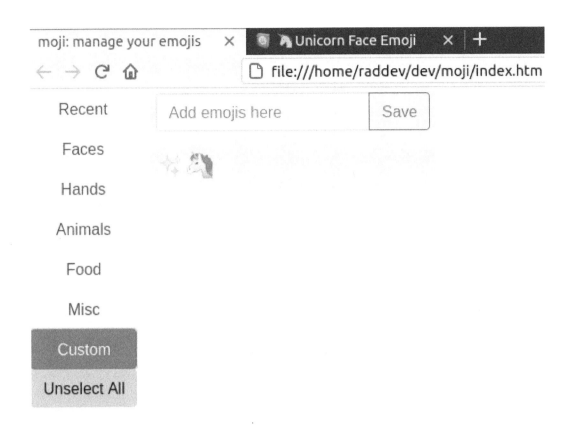

That's it for today. However, there are a couple of things we need to clean up to insure users are a bit more informed when they attempt to do things we don't want them to do (like add a duplicate custom emoji, or attempt to click the Save button when they haven't added any emojis). We'll wrap it up tomorrow and that will be all for Volume 2.

Day 54

NOTE: After I had almost completed today's entry, I learned there was a bug in the code. If you clicked emojis on the Custom or Recent tab nothing would happen (an error would appear in the Dev Console). The emoji would not be selected. Let's ignore this bug for now -- but I'll fix it and explain it at the end of today's entry and I'll update the code and save it in the moji-20 directory.

Just a few items to clean up and we will say goodbye in this Volume. But, do not worry! I will

be back with Volume 3 very soon. ☐ ☐

First of all, if the user does not add an emoji to the input text box and clicks the [Save] button then nothing really happens, but the user could get a bit confused.

Let's give her a message if this happens. And, let's not use a popup alert(), because those are actually annoying.

Instead, let's do this the Bootstrap way.

Bootstrap Alerts

Bootstrap uses Alerts which are simple panels which display a message in the main area of your app (instead of popping up).

You can see them at: https://getbootstrap.com/docs/5.0/components/alerts/

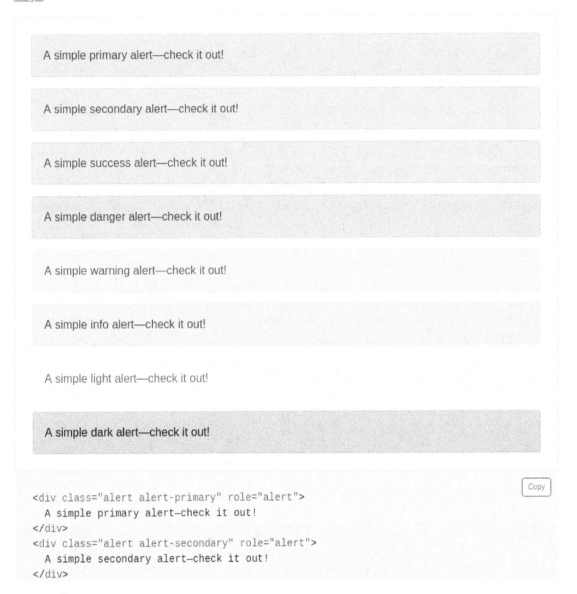

These panels are hidden in your HTML until you make them visible (when you need to alert the user to something in your app).

We have three different cases where we need to display a message to the user when she is attempting to add a Custom emoji.

1. Success - the emoji(s) were saved successfully

2. Nothing was added to the input box. Please add and try again.
3. Warning - One or more emojis were not added because it was a duplicate.

Here's the basic HTML that we add to add our three Alerts to our index.html. There are 3 main divs (one for each of our cases above) and each of those contain a message and close button

```
<div id="success-alert" class="alert alert-success alert-dismissible
fade show" role="alert">
   <strong>Success!</strong> The emoji(s) were successfully saved.
   <button type="button" onclick="dismiss('success-alert')"
class="btn-close"
         aria-label="Close"></button>
</div>
<div id="empty-alert" class="alert alert-warning alert-dismissible
fade show" role="alert">
    <strong>Warning! </strong>Please add an emoji and try again.
    <button onclick="dismiss('empty-alert')" type="button" class="btn-
close"
         aria-label="Close"></button>
 </div>
<div id="warn-alert" class="alert alert-warning alert-dismissible fade
show" role="alert">
     <strong>Warning!</strong> One ore more emoji(s) were not saved,
because they've
                         been added previously.
    <button onclick="dismiss('warn-alert')" type="button" class="btn-
close"
         aria-label="Close"></button>
  </div>
```

This all goes into the same <div> panel for our Custom tab.

If we add that code only, then all of the messages will appear by default.

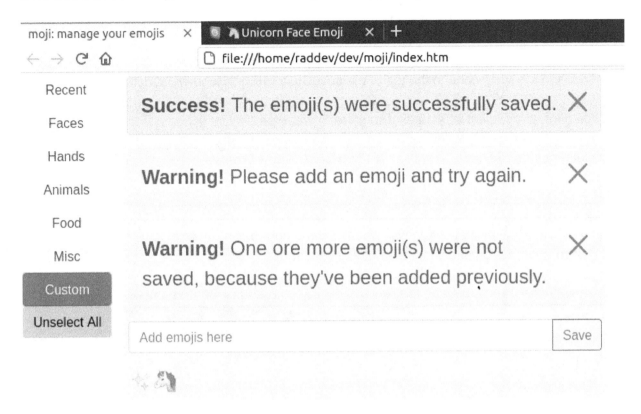

Of course, that isn't correct. We only want them to show when the related functionality fires and we need to inform the user.

Add CSS To Hide These By Default

We are going to add a very simple CSS style so these messages are hidden until they are used. This is the Bootstrap alert class so we will add the following code to our main.css:

.alert{font-size:small;display:none;visibility:hidden;}

Once you add that code and refresh, the messages will no longer appear.

Now we want them to appear when we choose.

For that we just need to alter our saveCustomEmojiHandler() method.

If User Clicks Save With Nothing in Input Box

First of all if the user clicks the [Save] button but there is nothing in the input text box then we want to warn her.

We'll add the following code to the top of the saveCustomEmojiHandler() function.

```
if (document.querySelector("#customEmojiText").value == ""){
    document.querySelector("#empty-alert").style.display = "block";
    document.querySelector("#empty-alert").style.visibility = "visible";
    return;
}
```

If the user clicks the [Save] button with no text in the input box then we display the message and exit (return) the function since there is nothing else to do.

You can see that I've also made the text smaller so the Alert is rendered smaller now.

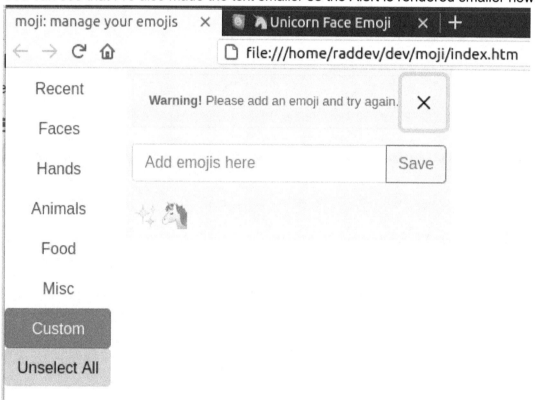

Of course the [X] close button does not work yet so until you refresh the page it will show up. That's not quite right.

Let's add the code so that when that button is clicked it will hide the message.

Just need to add the following new function to main.js:

```
function dismiss(target){
  document.querySelector(`#${target}`).style.display = "none";
  document.querySelector(`#${target}`).style.visibility = "hidden";
}
```

```
202    function dismiss(target){
203        document.querySelector(`#${target}`).style.display = "none";
204        document.querySelector(`#${target}`).style.visibility = "hidden";
205    }
```

This function takes the current element (alert message) and then applies a CSS style
dynamically to it. Actually it applies two styles : display: "none" and visibility: "hidden".
This effectively hides the alert.

Get the Code: Volume2\moji-19

Get the code and try this out.

Go to the Custom tab and click the [Save] button (insure there is nothing in the input box) and
you will see the Alert.

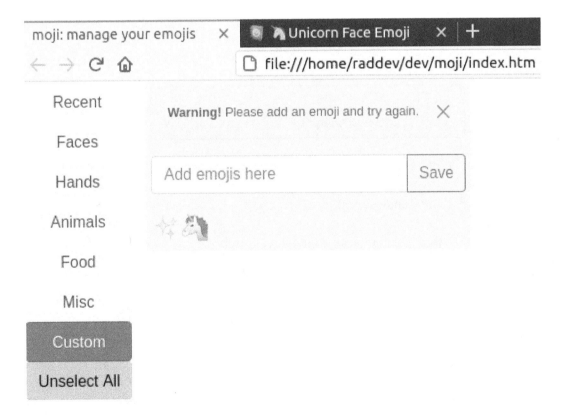

Click the [X] (close button) and you will see that the message disappears.

Emoji Click Problem: moji-20 Code Fix

I would end the day here but I noticed that I'd introduced a problem when I programmatically added these new elements via nodes. When you click an emoji on the Custom or Recent tab you may see an error (in the Dev Console - F12) that states:

```
Uncaught TypeError: Range.selectNodeContents: Argument 1 does not
implement interface Node.
```

Here's a snapshot of the error. Notice that it lists our functions which are firing in an effort to show us the chain of events. I must say this one was a bit of sticky wicket. But when I finally discovered the answer I was able to fix it with only three lines of code.

```
! ▶ Uncaught TypeError: Range.selectNodeContents: Argument 1 does not implement interface Node.
    displaySelectedElements              file:///home/raddev/dev/moji/js/main.js:147
    displaySelectedElements              file:///home/raddev/dev/moji/js/main.js:145
    handleEmojiClick                     file:///home/raddev/dev/moji/js/main.js:42
    displayCustomEmojis                  file:///home/raddev/dev/moji/js/main.js:191
    loadCustomEmojisFromLocalStorage file:///home/raddev/dev/moji/js/main.js:201
    loadCustomEmojisFromLocalStorage file:///home/raddev/dev/moji/js/main.js:200
    initApp                              file:///home/raddev/dev/moji/js/main.js:14
    onload                               file:///home/raddev/dev/moji/index.htm:1
! ▶ Uncaught TypeError: Range.selectNodeContents: Argument 1 does not implement interface Node.
    displaySelectedElements  file:///home/raddev/dev/moji/js/main.js:147
    displaySelectedElements  file:///home/raddev/dev/moji/js/main.js:145
    initApp                  file:///home/raddev/dev/moji/js/main.js:10
    initApp                  file:///home/raddev/dev/moji/js/main.js:10
    onload                   file:///home/raddev/dev/moji/index.htm:1
```

Because I know our code, I know that the root of all this is in handleEmojiClick() so I went there in order to discover what was going on. The first thing I did was do a console.log() of the el parameter that is passed into the handleEmojiClick() function.

You see, on the static emojis that call looks like the following (found in attachEmojiClickListeners):

handleEmojiClick(node);

Notice that we pass a node in when a static emoji is clicked.

However, later when we register that eventListener on our Custom and Recent emojis (which are both generated dynamically) it looks like the following:

newSpan.addEventListener("click", handleEmojiClick);

But notice that we just register the "click" event to point at the handleEmojiClick method but what is the parameter (el) that would be sent in??? I was a bit confused too.

So I added the console.log so I could see what the el parameter is when I click an emoji on the Recent or Custom tab.

console.log(el);

I made the handleEmojiClick method look like the following:

```
31    function handleEmojiClick(el) {
32        console.log(el);return;
```

This will just log the el to the console and then return out of the method. It's a nice little way to debug code.

Here's what I saw when I clicked one of the static emojis.

The output is a normal span element.

However, If clicked an emoji on the Recent or Custom tab I saw something different.

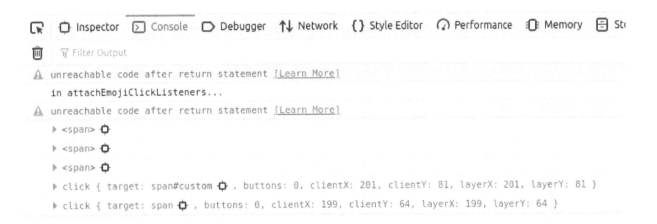

This is some other type of thing. I discovered that it is the actual click Event which is sent in. Luckily, you can see that there is a property of that Event named target (see more at : https://developer.mozilla.org/en-US/docs/Web/API/Event/target).

After I learned that, I went to our handleEmojiClick() function and I added the following three lines of code as the first three lines of the function.

```
if (el.target !== undefined){
    el = el.target;
```

}

Here's our entire handleEmojiClick function:

```
31   function handleEmojiClick(el) {
32       if (el.target !== undefined){
33         el = el.target;
34       }
35       if (isSelected(el)){
36           removeElement(el);
37       }
38       else{
39           allSelectedElements.push(el);
40           addEmojiToRecentList(el.innerHTML);
41       }
42       displaySelectedElements(el.innerHTML);
43   }
```

undefined: Special JavaScript Value

This code will check the item (el) sent into the function every time.
When it is a normal static element then the el.target will not exist : it is undefined.
When el.target doesn't exist (is undefined) then we don't have to do anything special.

When it is not undefined (!== undefined) which is difficult to say (and means that el.target is defined), then we want to set the value of el to el.target (the real element which is inside the Event object).

We set el to el.target because the thing we really want is the element that was clicked and the Event.target holds the element on which the event fired.

Now with this code everything works properly again and tomorrow we can finish up those other Alert messages.

Get the Code : Volume2\moji-20

Make sure you get the updated code so everything works for you.

Day 55

Right now, if you add a Custom emoji that you've already added, then the code will just return out of the method and not add it to the list. This is good, but it could confuse the user. Instead of just doing nothing, let's provide a message to the user also.

First of All: Let's Make Sure all Messages Are Cleared

Every time the user clicks the [Save] button, she is attempting the addition of a custom emoji so let's clear all the messages so old messages don't confuse her.

We'll just add the following code to the top of the Save button click handler.

```
dismiss("warn-alert");
dismiss("success-alert");
```

These two lines call our special dismiss method on the two alert divs and hides them. Very simple.

And finally, we just add the following code to show our messages each time the user adds a custom emoji.

```
if (atLeastOneFailure){
    document.querySelector("#warn-alert").style.display = "block";
    document.querySelector("#warn-alert").style.visibility = "visible";
  }
  else{
    // all successfully saved
    document.querySelector("#success-alert").style.display = "block";
    document.querySelector("#success-alert").style.visibility = "visible";
  }
```

Here's our entire saveCustomEmojiHandler() function with those lines at the bottom:

```
158    function saveCustomEmojiHandler(){
159      dismiss("warn-alert");
160      dismiss("success-alert");
161
162      if (document.querySelector("#customEmojiText").value == ""){
163        document.querySelector("#empty-alert").style.display = "block";
164        document.querySelector("#empty-alert").style.visibility = "visible";
165        return;
166      }
167      let allUserAddedEmojis = Array.from(document.querySelector("#customEmojiText").value);
168      document.querySelector("#customEmojiText").value = "";
169      let atLeastOneFailure = false;
170      for (let i = 0; i < allUserAddedEmojis.length;i++){
171        let emoji = allUserAddedEmojis[i];
172        if (isEmojiNew(emoji,customEmojis)){
173          // if it's new, push it onto the list and write to to localstorage
174          customEmojis.push(emoji);
175          localStorage.setItem("customEmojis", JSON.stringify(customEmojis));
176          displayCustomEmojis(emoji);
177        }
178        else{
179          atLeastOneFailure = true;
180        }
181        if (atLeastOneFailure){
182          document.querySelector("#warn-alert").style.display = "block";
183          document.querySelector("#warn-alert").style.visibility = "visible";
184        }
185        else{
186          // all successfully saved
187          document.querySelector("#success-alert").style.display = "block";
188          document.querySelector("#success-alert").style.visibility = "visible";
189        }
190      }
191    }
```

Everything works and we've fulfilled all of our User Stories on our backlog.
I added a new Lion emoji.

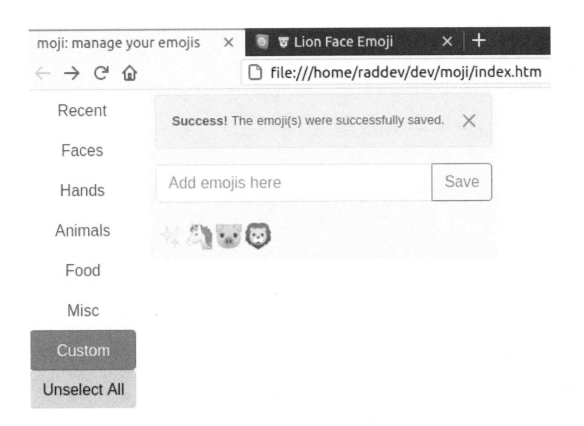

If I try to add the Lion emoji again I see the following:

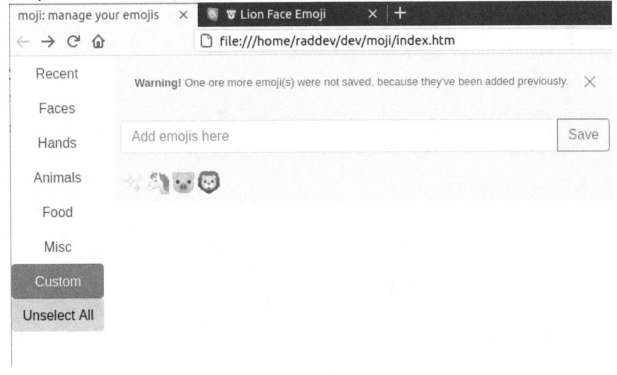

If the user adds multiple emojis at one time, and one or more of those have been previously added she will see this message also.

Get the Code: Volume2\emoji-21

Get the code and try it out.

Day 56

A few things to clean up and then we are done with this entire volume. You should be very proud because you have learned a lot of valuable things that will put you on the path to your development career.

1. **localStorage**
   a. how to clear it all, clear one item, etc. to clean it up for your testing.
2. **Move everything into initApp()**
   a. I forgot to move one addEventListener from the top of main.js so we'll move it from there to initApp().
3. **Add a XX-Large button** which allows user to toggle emoji sizes
4. **Is the App 100% Complete?**
   a. A note about possible bugs

1. localStorage Additional Items to Help Testing

I just wanted to mention a few more things about your localStorage.
You can clear all localStorage (for the current page -- file:/// or http://) with the following command in your dev console (F12) when you are viewing the page in your web browser:

> localStorage.clear()

That clears everything.
However, if you want to only clear the custom items you can use:

> localStorage.removeItem("customEmojis")

Or to clear all you recents use:

> localStorage.removeItem("recentEmojis")

2. Move Everything to initApp()

I forgot to move one item at the top of our main.js into the initApp() function so I'm going to do that now so everything is complete.

Moving Line 1 shown in the snapshot down into the initApp() function so it is the first line in initApp().

```js
JS main.js    X    <> index.htm       # main.css

js > JS main.js > ...
   1    addEventListener("load",attachEmojiClickListeners);
   2    const RECENTLY_USED_MAX = 50;
   3    let allSelectedElements = [];
   4    let recentlyUsedEmojis = [];
   5    let customEmojis = [];
   6
   7
   8    function initApp(){
   9        // this selector makes it so currently selected emojis are not unselected.
  10        document.querySelector("html").addEventListener("click", ()=>displaySelectedElements());
  11        document.querySelector("#saveCustomEmoji").addEventListener("click",saveCustomEmojiHandler);
  12
  13        loadRecentsFromLocalStorage();
  14        loadCustomEmojisFromLocalStorage();
  15    }
```

This simply cleans up everything so that all the initialization code is in one place and doesn't confuse us or another developer later if maintenance occurs on the app.

And, of course we don't need to do the call to addEvenListener("load") for this function now. Instead, we just call the attachEmojiClickListeners directly. The load is already being fired by the <body> tag which calls our initApp() function. Here's what our initApp() looks like now. It's just that one additional line which calls attachEmojiClickListeners().

```js
   7    function initApp(){
   8        attachEmojiClickListeners();
   9
  10        // this selector makes it so currently selected emojis are not unselected.
  11        document.querySelector("html").addEventListener("click", ()=>displaySelectedElements());
  12        document.querySelector("#saveCustomEmoji").addEventListener("click",saveCustomEmojiHandler);
  13
  14        loadRecentsFromLocalStorage();
  15        loadCustomEmojisFromLocalStorage();
  16    }
```

3. Add an XX-Large Button To Make Emojis Look Bigger

There's one more thing I wanted to do with the app to make it interesting.

I want to add a button that will make the emojis display at a larger size just so you can see the details in the emoji better. This change in size will not copy the size to the clipboard. Instead it will just make the emojis display larger.

Get the Final Code For Volume 2: moji-22

I'm adding the code for you into the final code drop for Volume 2 in moji-22.
You can take a look at it and see that you can toggle between the current size emojis and the XX-Large size. Here's a snapshot of the faces with XX-Large toggled on.

I've added a new value to localStorage which will remember which setting you had so it'll always display the way you last selected.

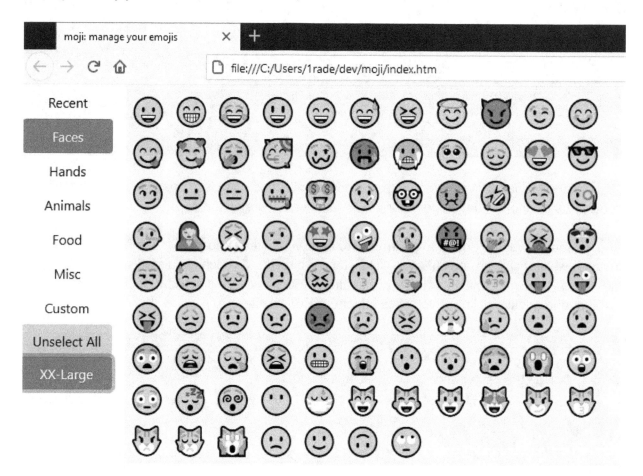

4. There Will Be Bugs

Warning! It is possible that the user can add other characters to their custom emojis which are not emojis. We haven't done anything to insure that doesn't happen. But checking the characters which are entered to determine if they are emojis or not is a somewhat difficult problem. Do a little research on what you might do and see what you think.

Of course there may be other unintended bugs also, but the app is fairly solid and can be quite useful. I actually use it quite often.

Selecting & Copying From Different Tabs

There are also some interesting things that go on when you select emojis on the various tabs. You will see that you can select one or more emojis from one or more tabs and they will stay selected. However, the copy function will only work on the emojis which are currently showing in the view. The emojis which are selected on tabs which are not displayed will not be copied. This is actually a kind of nice feature, but for others it may be annoying because they want to copy all emojis which are selected at once.

However, the [Unselect All] button does work on all tabs. That's because of the way we specify the unselect. These are just a couple of things to know about and change if you like.

Is the BackLog Complete?

Here's our original backlog again, with some notes.
- [X] As a user, I want to be able to select any emoji so I can add it to a document I am writing.
    - We completed this one throughout the work we did. This was one of our most important ones since it was part of the basic functionality required.
- [X] As a user, I want to be able to collect new emojis and add them into the program so I can use them later in documents I am writing.
    - This, of course, was our last item we worked on and we added valid messages to provide feedback to what the app does as the user attempts to add new emojis.
- [X]As a user, I want to be able to view my emojis in categories so I can find the one I want more easily.
    - This was one of the first things we did. This was an arbitrary grouping of emojis into various tabs which created categories. You can create more buttons and tabs and add more categories very easily and then each time the app loads it will assign all the eventListeners so clicking those emojis will work too.
- [X] As a user I want a list of my recently used emojis so I can find the one I want to use more easily.
    - This is a nice feature because you can quickly get to your most often used emojis instead of searching through the tabs for them.
- [X] As a user I want this program to run all the time on my desktop so I can easily copy an emoji and paste it into a document or post I am writing.

- ○ This one is solved simply by the user opening a new tab (or window) in her browser and leaving it open. This is how these abstract user stories are sometimes fulfilled. Later the entire team can discuss if this is a valid way to resolve it. For now, we have fulfilled this user story and consider it done.

The End: The Future

That's it for Volume 2, but I'll be back soon with Volume 3.

Web Site: http://LaunchYDC.com

I'm also building a website where I'll add links and new articles and release dates. Check it out. By the time you read this it will be there.

What will Volume 3 Cover?

At this point you understand how to build SPAs (Single Page Apps) which are all client-side (browser) code. Everything we've done has been to automate the browser. Even saving our data has been inside the browser (localStorage).

However, there are some things we just cannot do when we are limited to the browser. Some of those things we need a Server for. For example the localStorage data is only valid to your local browser. If you move to another machine or different web browser on the same machine you lose all your custom and recent emojis.

We need a way to save data on a remote server so the user can login and get her data from any device. This is going to require some understanding of Web Servers and how all that works.

In Volume 3 we'll begin to investigate how to set up our own web server and how to save data on the remote machine so it is available from anywhere. Some of this will touch on learning Web APIs.

That's it for now. Thanks for reading my book. I hope you learned a lot and it was enjoyable

See you at the web site and see you in Volume 3.
~Roger

```
Array.from(document.querySelectorAll("span")).map(element =>
element.addEventListener("click", function() {
  alert(element.innerHTML);
}));
```